# JUDGES AND JURORS: THEIR FUNCTIONS, QUALIFICATIONS AND SELECTION

BOSTON UNIVERSITY • The Gaspar G. Bacon Lectures
on the Constitution of the United States

# JUDGES AND JURORS: THEIR FUNCTIONS, QUALIFICATIONS AND SELECTION

by
ARTHUR T. VANDERBILT
*The Chief Justice*
Supreme Court of New Jersey

Boston University Press
Boston, Massachusetts
1958

COPYRIGHT
THE TRUSTEES OF BOSTON UNIVERSITY, 1956
Second Printing, 1958

KF
8775
.V35

LIBRARY OF CONGRESS CATALOG CARD NO. 56-9547

*Lithographed by the*
Boston Blue Print Company
*Lithographic Division*
Boston, Massachusetts, U.S.A.

BU 2-58

# FOREWORD

The Gaspar G. Bacon Lectureship on the Constitution of the United States was established in 1927 by Mrs. Robert Bacon of New York in honor of her son, at that time Secretary of the Board of Trustees of Boston University. After several terms in the Massachusetts State Legislature and two years as lieutenant-governor, Gaspar G. Bacon retired from active politics and joined the faculty of Boston University in the department of Government in 1938. His teaching career was interrupted by four years of service in World War II, which he foresaw well in advance of his fellow countrymen. His experience in politics, his brilliant record as Lieutenant-Colonel in Military Government in the European theatre, followed by a year of travel in South America and a year teaching at the University of North Carolina, were varied experiences which he hoped to share with students on his return to Boston University in September 1947. He died suddenly on Christmas Day, 1947. By gift and bequest he augmented the fund established by his mother and thus made possible publication of the lectures which bear his name. He himself inaugurated the series in 1927. Since that time lectures have been given annually by some eminent scholar or jurist in fulfillment of the terms of the deed of gift which reads, "The purpose of the Lectureship is to stimulate a study of the Constitution of the United States, its antecedents, history and doctrines, together with the results and implications thereof."

Arthur T. Vanderbilt, the Chief Justice of the Supreme Court of New Jersey, gave the Bacon Lectures for 1954-55. His general subject, "Judges and Jurors: Their Functions, Qualifications and Selection", was treated in three separate lectures "The Judicial Office and the Judicial Function", "Qualifications and Selection of Judges", and "The Functions, Qualifications and Selection of Jurors", delivered on February 15, 16 and 17, 1955 respectively. Chief Justice Vanderbilt re-examines the qualifications and rôle of the "decision-makers" who administer justice through our courts. The court system of the State of New Jersey has been reorganized largely under the guidance and direction of Chief Justice Vanderbilt, long an exponent of a fairer and more efficient administration of justice. This series of lectures will be of special interest to citizens of Massachusetts in considering the report of Governor Herter's Judicial Survey Commission which recommends improvements in administration of the court system in Massachusetts

# PREFACE

The Gaspar G. Bacon Lectureship was established at Boston University in 1927 "to stimulate a study of the Constitution of the United States, its antecedents, history and doctrines, together with the results and implications thereof." This is in the best Anglo-American tradition—as advocated in the fifteenth century by Fortescue, reiterated in the eighteenth century by Blackstone and accepted in this country by James Wilson—that a liberal education is enhanced by an understanding of the fundamental institutions of the law. In the universal ferment of today attention is being increasingly focused on the study of law as a discipline because of its basic importance in a world in which governmental functions are continually expanding. More than ever the question is being asked whether a person can be said to be educated who lacks, to quote Blackstone, "a competent knowledge of the laws of that society in which we live."[1]

In three brief hours I have attempted to develop, primarily for graduate students in government but also with the general reader in mind, some understanding of the bases of the judicial process so that they may better comprehend the functioning of a government operating under a written Constitution and the workings of the judicial system under which we live.

The judicial process is not something apart from life. Our system of judicial administration has developed out of the experience and the needs of free people. While it is largely the work of a relatively small group of men—judges, lawyers, legislators and the authors of our legal classics—it is only through the assistance of the intelligently educated laymen who understand how important it is for our courts to have the confidence of the public, that essential improvements can be made. In these unsettled days when every good citizen should be giving thought to how best to preserve individual freedom while at the same time strengthening the processes of government, it seems to me that the solution of the problem of improving the caliber of those who administer justice has an immediacy that cannot be denied. The public is only too well aware of this, but it is unable to offer suggestions until it understands better the judicial functions, judicial qualifications, and the relation of judge and jurors. For this some knowledge of the history and purpose of these institutions is essential. As Woodrow Wilson said in 1894, "Nothing will steady us like a body of citizens instructed in the essential nature and processes of law . . . We need laymen who under-

---

[1] Book 1, Sec. 1, par. 5-6.

stand the necessity for law and the right uses of it too well to be unduly impatient of its restraints."[2]

It is in the courts, and not at the hands of the executive or the Legislature that our citizens feel the keen edge of the law, and they therefore judge the law by what they see and hear in court, and by the character and manners of judges, and by what they are called upon to do as jurors, quite as much as by the rules of law alone. Only if the citizen clearly understands the functions of a judge, the importance of a fair trial, the purposes of appellate review, and the philosophy underlying the judicial office, can the true value of the rule of law in safeguarding individual liberty be understood. When the essential characteristics of judicial office—impartiality, independence and immunity—are pointed out and the attributes of a good judge indicated, the principle that the selection of judges should be divorced from political considerations becomes self-evident. Only if those who are to act as jurors understand the role of lay personnel in the administration of justice do the standards for the qualification and selection of jurors as well as the relation of judge and jury become meaningful.

The problem of popular education in these institutions and their related procedures is an important one which cannot be neglected in a free society, for a "critical understanding of legal processes and institutions in a democracy helps to make free men wise."[3] It is as true today as it was when the nation was first established that "The knowledge of those rational principles on which the law is founded, ought, especially in a free government, to be diffused over the whole community."[4]

---

[2] 17 A.B.A. Rep. 439, 440-441 (1894).
[3] Currie, *The Place of Law in the Liberal Arts College*, 5 J. of Leg. Ed. 428, 437 (1953).
[4] James Wilson, *Lectures in Law*, 9-10 (1804).

# CONTENTS

| | PAGE |
|---|---|
| 1. *The Importance of Courts and Their Personnel:* | |
| Court's role in preservation of internal peace | 1 |
| Importance of caliber of courts' personnel | 2 |
| 2. *The Functions of Judges:* | |
| Decision of particular disputes | 3 |
| Adjustment and development of the common law | 4 |
| Responsibilities of the trial judge | 5 |
| Restrictions on common law powers of trial judges | 6 |
| Duties in trial without a jury | 8 |
| Discretion and responsibility in ruling on post trial motions | 9 |
| Finality of decisions of trial judge | 10 |
| Judicial review of statutes, determination of questions of constitutionality | 10 |
| Judicial regulation of procedure | 11 |
| Administrative duties of judges | 12 |
| Non-Judicial assignments for judges | 12 |
| 3. *The Rule of Law and the Development of the Anglo-American Judicial Office:* | |
| Anglo-American philosophy of judicial office | 13 |
| Achievement of the rule of law | 14 |
| Historical development of judicial office in England | 15 |
| Securing judicial tenure during good behavior | 17 |
| Judicial independence and the rule of law | 18 |
| 4. *The Essential Characteristics of Judicial Office:* | |
| Impartiality | 19 |
| Independence and Immunity | 20 |
| 5. *Tenure of Judicial Office and an Independent Judiciary:* | |
| American colonial complaint of uncertain judicial tenure | 21 |
| Original acceptance of tenure during good behavior | 22 |
| Present limited judicial tenure in the states | 24 |
| Relation between judicial tenure and judicial independence | 25 |
| II. THE ATTRIBUTES AND THE SELECTION OF JUDGES | 26 |
| 1. *Attributes of a Good Judge:* | |
| Professional learning | 27 |
| Canons of Judicial Ethics, standards for judicial behavior | 28 |
| Requirements of character, intellect, knowledge and human relations | 30 |
| Difficulties of formulating objective standards | 31 |

## CONTENTS

PAGE

2. *Selection of Judges:*
   *In England,* methods and high standards ............ 32
   *In America,* the federal courts ..................... 35
   Jacksonian revolution and popular election of state judges 36
   Ad interim appointments improving caliber of elected judges ............................................. 37
   Partisan political influence on judicial selection in United States ............................................. 38
   Bipartisan judicial appointments .................... 39
   Politics and elected judiciary ....................... 40
   Chicago experience .................................. 41
   Difficulties of electorate in selecting judges ............ 42
   Partisan pressures of elective system or lessening judicial independence ...................................... 43
   Elimination of political influences from judicial selection 45
   American Bar Association plan to improve judicial selection ............................................... 46
   *On the continent,* judicial profession, selection and promotion ............................................. 47
   *The Appropriate Method,* for judicial selection, relation to local needs and practices ....................... 47
   Need to establish basic qualifications as an aid in selection 48
   Advantage of bipartisan judiciary ................... 49
   Common law tradition of judicial independence and the selection of good judges ........................... 50

III. THE FUNCTIONS, QUALIFICATIONS AND SELECTION OF JURORS ................................................. 51

1. *The Functions of Jurors:*
   Common law jury trial, destructiveness of ............ 51
   Jury origins ........................................ 51
   Importance of grand jury ........................... 52
   Bushell's Case and development of trial jury's independence ............................................. 53
   Jurors' decision of question of fact .................. 54
   Common law trial development ..................... 55
   Popularity of jury trial in America .................. 56
   Essential elements of jury trial ...................... 57
   American trend to enlargen scope of jury decision ...... 58
   Effect of restriction on judge's powers to instruct jury .. 59
   Contrast between English and American jury practices .. 60
   Proper allocation of respective functions between judge and jury .......................................... 61

2. *Qualifications of Jurors:*
   Common law and present English ................... 62
   Impartiality ........................................ 63
   Studies of American jurors ......................... 64
   Standards for appraisal of qualifications of jurors ...... 65
   State practice as to qualifications of jurors ............ 65
   Variety of exemptions from jury service .............. 66

## CONTENTS

PAGE

3. *Selection of Juries:*
   Evil of political influence on .......................... 67
   Recommendation for selection by jury commissioners appointed by judges .............................. 68
   Methods of selecting jury panels ................... 69
   Examination on voir dire .......................... 71
   Challenges and their use .......................... 72
   English practices ................................. 72
   Contrast in conduct of voir dire by judges and attorneys  73

4. *Status of Jury in England and United States:*
   Decline of use of jury in England .................. 74
   Criticism of juries in United States ................ 75
   Recommendations for improvement in jury practice and proper allocation of function between judge and jury.. 76

# JUDGES AND JURORS: THEIR FUNCTIONS, QUALIFICATIONS AND SELECTION

## I

### THE OFFICE AND FUNCTIONS OF A JUDGE

#### 1. The Importance of Courts and Their Personnel

First let me point out the place of the courts in the broad field of government.

There are two fundamental functions of government in every state that hopes to survive. The first of these two fundamental functions is the preservation of the state and its citizens from external dangers— dangers that are never far from our minds these troublesome times. These dangers include war and threats of war. They may be intellectual, emotional or spiritual dangers quite as much as physical. With these external dangers the courts have little to do directly.

The second fundamental function of every state is to preserve itself and its citizens from internal dangers. These internal dangers, like external dangers, may be either physical or mental. The state must protect itself from internal breaches of the peace ranging from simple assault and battery to treason. It must also prevent any undermining of the social order and at the same time it must keep open the avenues of social progress, including the adjudication of disputes between citizens.

In the process of preserving the state internally the courts play a prominent, although not an exclusive part.[1] They provide the instrumentality for the trial of disputes between individuals and between the state and individuals for the protection of human beings living in organized society. A court is a tribunal presided over by a judge or judges exercising power conferred by law and deciding cases according to law.

While the courts play the predominant part in the administration of both civil and criminal justice, they must call on the executive branch of government to enforce their orders and on the legislative department

---

[1] Laski, *The Judicial Functions*, POLITICA 115 at 116, 118, 124 (Nov. 1936).

to appropriate the funds for their operation. Despite the existence of the courts as one of the three coordinate parts of the government, as Alexander Hamilton put it in *The Federalist* papers:

> "The judiciary ... has no influence over either the sword or the purse; no direction either of the strength or of the wealth of the society; and can take no active resolution whatever. It may truly be said to have neither FORCE nor WILL, but merely judgment.... The judiciary is beyond comparison the weakest of the three departments ..."[2]

These weaknesses constitute the very strength of the courts and of the judiciary for if they are to retain public respect and confidence they must remain aloof from the struggles both of the battlefield and of the legislative forum.

In the many competing interests and ambitions of men in daily life the courts strive to substitute reason and justice for force and fraud. The fundamental consideration in every court is manifestly the caliber of its personnel. The law as administered cannot be better than the judge who expounds it, the jurors who find the facts under the instructions of the judge as to the law, and the lawyers who try the case. Each must fulfill his function properly or a miscarriage of justice may ensue. The courts operate largely through judges and jurors, and accordingly it is with the work of judges and jurors that we shall deal, although we are not unmindful of the importance of the tasks performed in the administration of justice by lawyers and other officers of the courts. In the Anglo-American legal system judges are not public servants in the same sense as are officials of the executive. They must often decide delicate issues between the government and private parties[3] and so must be considered as public employees who are independent of the government of which they are indeed an integral part.[4] The character and personality of the judge are of critical importance. The personnel who fill that office control the processes of trial, the successful determination of disputes, the enforcement of the law, and the interpretation of the constitution. Even in those instances where a judge does not make law his manner of conduct of a trial may determine its outcome. This is indeed a "government of laws and not of men", but the adminis-

---

[2] No. 78 at 519 (Ford ed. 1898).
[3] See statement of Chief Justice Marshall quoted at n. 85 *infra*.
[4] See ROBSON, JUSTICE AND ADMINISTRATIVE LAW 42 (2d ed. 1947): "The judiciary is, in effect, part of the public service of the Crown. But a judge is not 'employed' in the sense that a civil servant is employed. He fills a public office, which is by no means the same thing; and part of his independence consists in the fact that no one can give him orders as to the manner in which he is to perform his work...." To a similar effect see Holdsworth, *The Constitutional Position of the Judge*, 48 L.Q. REV. 25 (1932).

tration and enforcement of those laws are in the hands of men,[5] for as Chief Judge Learned Hand has said:

> "a government of laws without men is as visionary as a government of men without laws; the solution will always be a compromise based on experience."[6]

The judicial task has many facets and the duties and functions of the judges are far from simple. Recognition that large discretionary powers should be vested in the court to control its procedure and the management of its business presupposes the selection of able, experienced, conscientious and unbiased judges. Improvement of judicial organization and of court procedure is most essential but the relation of the character of the judiciary to these considerations cannot be overestimated. The best organization of the courts will be ineffective, if the judges who man it are lacking in the necessary qualifications. A court cannot exist without a judge and proper administrative supervision of the judicial system as a whole by an able judiciary is of much importance in helping the judge in his fundamental task of administering justice.

The judge is indeed indispensable to our notion of a court, but under our constitutional guarantees the trial judge cannot in many instances act without the assistance of a jury.[7] The functions of jurors, their qualification and selection, their relationship to the judge are of vital importance in effectuating the administration of justice. Judges and jurors are the structural components through which the Anglo-American legal system was developed and on which it rests.

### 2. The Functions of Judges

What are the functions of a judge? His first duty is to decide controversies between individuals or between the state and individuals that come before him in the regular course of his official duties in court. In doing so in the ordinary case the trial judge merely applies the known law to the facts as he finds them, or, if he is sitting with a jury, he instructs the jury on the law of the case, leaving it to them to find the

---

[5] See Hernandez v. Texas, 347 U.S. 475 (1954), in which petitioner alleged that persons of Mexican descent were systematically excluded from jury service, although there were such persons qualified to serve. The Court, per Chief Justice Warren, recognized that: "As the petitioner acknowledges, the Texas system of selecting grand and petit jurors by the use of jury commissions is fair on its face and capable of being utilized without discrimination." At 478-479. But it upheld petitioner's allegation that those who administered the law were employing the system in a discriminatory manner, concluding that: "The result bespeaks discrimination, whether or not it was a conscious decision on the part of any individual jury commissioner." At 482.

[6] *The Deficiencies of Trials to Reach the Heart of the Matter*, in 3 LECTURES ON LEGAL TOPICS, 1921-1922 (Assn. of the Bar of the City of N.Y. 1926) at 89, 102.

[7] See Lecture III *infra* at pp. 51-62.

facts and to apply the law as charged by him to the facts as found by them. Because of the danger that a single judge may misstate the law, especially in an unusual case, provision is made for the review by an appellate court of the trial court's rulings and judgment. Such review aims not merely at the correction of error in the interest of justice; it does more. The opinion handed down on the appeal fixes the law on the question before the reviewing court; the trial judges are required to follow the rulings of the reviewing court in all succeeding cases. But, although the trial judges are bound by the doctrine of precedent (stare decisis) to follow the decisions of the appellate courts, they can, and good trial judges regularly do, assist the appellate court by making suggestions in their opinions as to the desirability of changes in the law to meet the requirements of a case pending before them.

In the unusual case, involving some novel situation of fact, judges will generally reason by analogy from cases resembling the controversy before them. Even though their reasoning be by analogy and hence inductive in nature, they have a way of stating their decisions in terms of deductive logic as if their conclusions were drawn from universal principles. By this process of analyzing the facts, reasoning by analogy and then stating their conclusions as deductions from broad pre-existing principles, judges are enabled not only to decide the controversy pending before them but to aid in the growth of the law to meet new situations of fact in a changing world. Thus the decision in any given controversy not only disposes of the case, but states the rule that will govern in future cases of the same sort. Accordingly, it will be seen that judicial reasoning is by no means the judges' own personal thinking alone. They are concerned with the problem before them in the light of the law that has been developed in earlier cases and with due regard to related cases that may arise in the future. For example, Lord Chief Justice Coke stated the law correctly for his time when he told us that the owner of a piece of land has rights not only in the surface of his land but downward to the center of the earth and upward indefinitely into the sky. The use of the airwaves in wireless telegraphy, in operating the radio and television, and the advent of the airplane above the surface of the land posed new problems that have forced a change in this ancient rule of law to meet today's new conditions.[8]

The usual case presents a dispute simply as to the facts and no difficulties of law, but the responsibilities of judges in the unusual cases

---

[8] PROSSER, HANDBOOK OF THE LAW OF TORTS 85-88 (1941). See id. n. 68 for citation of discussions of the property rights in airspace. See also, Richardson, *Private Property Rights in the Air Space at Common Law*, 31 CAN. B. REV. 117 (1953); Notes, 37 MARQ. L. REV. 176 (1953); 20 N.Y.U.L. REV. 169 (1954).

that involve changing conditions cannot be overestimated; as Chief Judge Learned Hand puts it:

> "the customary law of English-speaking peoples stands, a structure indubitably made by the hands of generations of judges, each professing to be a pupil, yet each in fact a builder who has contributed his few bricks and his little mortar, often indeed under the delusion that he has added nothing. A judge must manage to escape both horns of this dilemma: he must preserve his authority by cloaking himself in the majesty of an overshadowing past; but he must discover some composition with the dominant trends of his time—at all hazards he must maintain that tolerable continuity without which society dissolves, and men must begin again the weary path up from savagery."[9]

By this process repeated by judges century after century the common law has been built up into one of the world's great legal systems,[10] which is continually being adjusted through the mediation of the judiciary to the needs of the times, though necessarily always lagging somewhat behind the demand for change. Although a considerable part of our law consists of statutes and constitutions, the amount of judge-made law or common law is far more extensive than is popularly realized. The law reports contain the facts of the cases as summarized by the judges and the reasons given for coming to a particular decision. These judicial opinions of appellate courts[11] embody the precedents that compose the common law, and that govern whole fields of law and the myriads of situations to which legislation does not apply. The Restatements of the Law of the American Law Institute[12] bear witness to the wide sphere of the common law even in an era of great legislative activity.

While the appellate court consists of several judges—usually three, five, seven or nine—in this country the trial judge customarily sits alone and his position is one of great responsibility. On his demeanor and conduct the atmosphere of the courtroom depends. A weak judge may allow a trial to be disturbed by spectators or may permit unseemly conduct by lawyers, parties, witnesses or the public. A trial is a serious

---

[9] HAND, THE SPIRIT OF LIBERTY 130 (Dilliard ed. 1953).
[10] Holdsworth, *The Constitutional Position of the Judge*, 48 L.Q. REV. 25, 32 (1932).
[11] Dean Roscoe Pound observed: "When it comes to the judges of the appellate courts, we entrust them with a power over law making that exists nowhere else on earth." *The Judicial Office in America*, 10 B.U.L. REV. 125, 134 (1930). He has also pointed out that in the period from the establishment of the United States to the Civil War it was often less important for judges to decide a particular case justly than to settle the law. THE FORMATIVE ERA OF AMERICAN LAW 103 (1938).
[12] See AMERICAN LAW INSTITUTE RESTATEMENT IN THE COURTS 9-11 (1944). Restatements have been published for AGENCY, CONFLICT OF LAWS, CONTRACTS, JUDGMENTS, PROPERTY, RESTITUTION, SECURITY, TORTS, AND TRUSTS.

matter and proper behavior in the courtroom is controlled by the trial judge. Of the three lawyers in the courtroom he alone is personally disinterested in the outcome of the case. His rulings as to legality determine the admissibility of evidence. In many classes of cases, such as equity, admiralty and bankruptcy matters, he sits alone and is the sole judge of both the law and the facts. When he sits with a jury he not only instructs them with respect to the law of the case, but if the verdict of the jury is contrary to the evidence he has the power to set aside the verdict and grant a new trial.

At a trial the efficiency of which is determined in large measure by the extent of the judge's authority in relation to the jury and to counsel for the litigants, the judge should be the dominant figure. His power to control the conduct of the case and to comment to the jury on the weight and credibility of the evidence, analyzing and summarizing it, were essential parts of a jury trial at common law.[13] If necessary in the interest of justice he interrogated the witness and after counsel had made their closing arguments to the jury he charged the jury in his own language so that his words were fresh in the jurors' minds when they retired to consider their verdict. His powers at common law, however, were not unlimited:

> "The privilege of the judge to comment on the facts has its inherent limitations. His discretion is not arbitrary and uncontrolled, but judicial, to be exercised in conformity with the standards governing the judicial office. . . . He may analyze and dissect the evidence, but he may not either distort it or add to it."[14]

And the trial judge must, of course, plainly and emphatically instruct the jury that they are the sole judges of the facts of a case and that, if their recollection of the facts varies from his, it is their recollection, not his, that is to govern them. In short, the judge may aid the jury but not seek to control them.

Although the movement commenced earlier,[15] it was primarily in the nineteenth century that the judicial power of the trial judge in this country was drastically curtailed in many American states.[16] As the power of the trial judge decreased, the role of the advocates became

---

[13] See HALE, THE HISTORY OF THE COMMON LAW 291-292 (4th ed. 1792); Otis, *The Judge to the Jury*, 6 KAN. CITY L. REV. 1, 14-15 (1937).

[14] Quercia v. United States, 289 U.S. 466, 470, 53 S.Ct. 698, 77 L.Ed. 1321 (1933).

[15] See Wright, *Instructions to the Jury: Summary Without Comment*, 1954 WASH. U.L.Q. 177, 193, 196 for discussion of North Carolina statute and Tennessee constitutional provision of 1796.

[16] MILLAR, CIVIL PROCEDURE OF THE TRIAL COURT IN HISTORICAL PERSPECTIVE 310-315 (1952). See as to effects of such curtailment of judicial power, STOREY, REFORM OF LEGAL PROCEDURE 98-122 (1911). For reasons leading to the imposition of such restrictions see *e.g.* Pound, *The Judicial Office in America*, 10 B.U.L. REV. 123 (1930); Note, 27 N. DAK. L. REV. 199 (1951).

dominant, and a trial instead of being an attempt to discover the truth generally became a battle of wits between opposing counsel.[17] The judge's duties and powers were limited in such jurisdictions by requiring that the judge's instructions to the jury precede the summations by counsel. The instructions, moreover, were not to be given in the judge's own language, but he was required to read from requests submitted to him by one or another or both of the lawyers in the case. These instructions were couched in legalistic language and the judge was not permitted to explain or clarify their meaning. The influence of instructions under such conditions must be negligible.[18] The judge was not allowed to sum up the evidence or comment on the facts developed during the trial, but was confined, as it was generally put, to comments on the law. In the absence of proper explanation jurors who were untrained in law and unaccustomed to trial procedure were frequently confused by occurrences and rulings at the trial and by arguments of counsel that might not have been strictly relevant to the issues of the case. Indeed, they might not even have remembered all the evidence that was presented. Therefore it is of prime importance that the judge be able to control the conduct of the counsel at the trial and to give to the jury a clear and impartial summing up of the evidence, pointing out the questions at issue, and commenting upon the relevant evidence.[19]

---

[17] For early recognition of this, see speech by Henry Billings Brown (later Associate Justice of the United States Supreme Court, 1891-1906) before the American Bar Association in 1889. *Judicial Independence,* 12 A.B.A. REP. 265, 275 (1889). He pointed out that statutes curtailing the common law prerogative of the judges tended "to strengthen the power of the ablest counsel and correspondingly to weaken that of the less experienced. . . ." He also indicated: "In my view a judge ought to be something more than a mere umpire. He should bear in mind that the sole object of our judicial machinery is to secure exact justice between the parties in each case, and that he has no right to sit quietly by and see a manifest wrong done, simply because young or inexperienced counsel have overlooked or misapprehended a vital point. . . . The whole inquiry, then, resolves itself into this simple question: What are the proper functions of the judge? If they are limited to deciding questions as they arise and declaring the law to the jury, then it is right that the whole burden of the trial should be assumed by counsel; but if, upon the other hand, the responsibility is with the judge, and counsel are employed to assist him in administering justice, and the jury are the legal advisers of the court, authorized only to pass upon questions of fact, concerning which there is some real conflict in the testimony, then it is not only his right, but in some cases his duty to act as their friend and counsellor." *Id.* at 275-276.

[18] MORGAN, CHAFFEE, GIFFORD, HINTON, HOUGH, JOHNSTON, SUNDERLAND, WIGMORE, THE LAW OF EVIDENCE, SOME PROPOSALS FOR ITS REFORM 9-21 (1927); Wright, *Instructions to the Jury: Summary Without Comment,* 1954 WASH. U.L.Q. 177.

[19] *Instructions to Jurors, Report of a Committee of the Section of Judicial Administration of the American Bar Association,* 10 F.R.D. 409, 411 (1949); Note, 27 N. DAK. L. REV. 199, 205 (1951). THE MODEL CODE OF EVIDENCE OF THE AMERICAN LAW INSTITUTE (1942) embodies a provision for the return to the orthodox common law rule as to the powers of the trial judge. Rule 8. See *id.* at 13, 15, 81.

Criticism of the jury as a fact-finding agency has been due to a large extent to the fact that the lawyers have been given too much leeway, the jury too much responsibility, and the trial judge too little in many of our states.

The trial judge's power and practice of commenting to the jury on the evidence has been an essential part of a jury trial for centuries. In many states today the judge is prohibited from even summarizing the evidence, and only in the federal courts and one quarter of our state courts is the trial judge permitted to comment on the weight of the evidence in accordance with the common law practice.[20] In many states the judge, stripped of these important functions, has shrunk to the position of a mere moderator. His lessened control over the conduct of a jury trial has worked to the detriment of all concerned in the achievement of a just decision. Where these heresies are found, they cast a very dark shadow on the administration of justice, for complete justice cannot be administered by a judge in fetters. Fortunately, this situation does not prevail in the federal courts or in a considerable number of states or anywhere else in the common law world.[21] That it has continued here in so many states for more than a century is a grave reflection on every branch of the legal profession—judge, practitioner and law professor—for in each such state there is at hand the opportunity for a daily comparison of the trial methods of the federal courts and of the state courts.

In those cases where a jury trial is not authorized or is waived, the entire trial is conducted by the judge. In such instances the judge must not only apply the law, but determine the facts. If the trial judge is to do his job well he must use every bit of his experience and should, if possible, elicit any relevant additional facts so as to determine the truth behind what are often conflicting stories of witnesses. In the federal courts in civil cases tried without a jury the judge is required to summarize the facts of the case as he finds them and the conclusions of law which are the basis of his judgment.[22] Thus the judge may not give judgment unless he has carefully analyzed the facts and the issues litigated and has formulated the reasons for his decision.[23]

---

[20] VANDERBILT, MINIMUM STANDARDS OF JUDICIAL ADMINISTRATION 227-234 (1949). For results of recent careful examination of relevant practices, see Curtis Wright, Jr., *Instructions to the Jury: Summary Without Comment*, 1954 WASH. U.L.Q. 177; *Adequacy of Instructions to the Jury*, 53 MICH. L. REV. 813 (1955); *The Invasion of Jury: Temperature of the War*, 27 TEMP. L.Q. 137 (1953).

[21] For an interesting argument that the judge was an indispensable factor of a jury trial at common law and that therefore just as the jury is, he is entitled "to protection against legislative interference in the discharge of his common law duties," see Brown, *supra* note 17, at 272.

[22] Fed. Rules Civ. Proc. 52(a). Cf. Fed. Rule Crim. Proc. 23(c). See Note, 61 HARV. L. REV. 1434 (1948) as to operation of Civil Rule 52(a).

[23] See as to a judge's difficulties in trying a case without a jury and his need

The final task of the trial judge is to give judgment in a civil case, to sentence a defendant found guilty in a criminal case,[24] and to rule on various motions relating to the jury's verdict, for correction of the judgment or for a new trial.[25] A trial judge has a wide discretion in awarding a new trial when for some reason he believes justice requires a new trial.[26] The judge's responsibility at this point is particularly great. Thus he may order a new trial because he considers the jury's verdict finding the defendant guilty of murder in the first degree was not supported by substantial evidence so that a miscarriage of justice has resulted.[27] Again, in a civil case he may deny a motion for a new trial on the condition that the successful party release a portion of the verdict considered by the judge to be excessive.[28] In some jurisdictions a trial judge may, despite a jury recommendation of life imprisonment, sentence the defendant to death.[29] The court may also enter a judgment of acquittal despite the jury verdict that a defendant is guilty when the judge is himself convinced of the defendant's innocence.[30] In these tasks, as in the entire judicial process, the trial judge is entrusted with the power of making very important decisions, decisions which because of their finality have a solemnity which requires of the judge the utmost searching of his conscience.[31]

In considering the work of the trial judge we must bear in mind that all but the merest fraction of his decisions—perhaps one per cent at the

---

to explain his decisions to counsel, BOK, BACKBONE OF THE HERRING 194-201 (1941). See also, Frank, *Both Ends Against the Middle*, 100 U. PA. L. REV. 20, 37-42 (1951); Hutcheson, *The Judgment Intuitive: The Function of the "Hunch" in Judicial Decision*, 14 CORNELL L.Q. 274 (1929); Wyzanski, *A Trial Judge's Freedom and Responsibility*, 65 HARV. L. REV. 1281, 1293-1297 (1952).

[24] As to extent of judicial discretion see ORFIELD, CRIMINAL PROCEDURE FROM ARREST TO APPEAL 548-570 (1947). See also as to Massachusetts practice and suggestion of a disposition tribunal to exercise the sentencing function, WARNER & CABOT, JUDGES AND LAW REFORM 156-180 (1936).

[25] See Fed. Rules Civ. Proc. 50, 59, 60; MILLAR, *op. cit. supra* n. 16, at 385-408; FEDERAL RULES CRIM. PROC. 29, 33, 34-36; ORFIELD, *op. cit. supra* n. 24, at 498-570.

[26] See BOK, *op. cit. supra* n. 23, at 201-202.

[27] United States v. Parelius, 83 F. Supp. 617 (D. Hawaii, 1949).

[28] Rice v. Union Pacific R. Co., 82 F. Supp. 1002 (D. Neb. 1949). An increase in the amount of damages awarded by the jury when the judge considers the damages inadequate is not allowed in the federal courts as a condition of a denial of a motion for new trial. Dimick v. Schiedt, 293 U.S. 474, 55 S.Ct. 296, 79 L.Ed. 603 (1934). As to the policy of the states in allowing remittitur see MINIMUM STANDARDS *op. cit. supra* n. 20, at 245-246.

[29] See Williams v. New York, 337 U.S. 241, 69 S.Ct. 1079, 93 L.Ed. 1337 (1949). In this case the judge's consideration of evidence not developed at the trial but included in a presentence investigation in determining the sentence was upheld. See also People of Virgin Islands v. Price, 181 F.2d 394 (3rd Cir. 1950) indicating that a jury's recommendation of the death sentence was not conclusive and that the judge, although giving due consideration to such recommendation, must determine the sentence independently.

[30] United States v. Gardiner, 171 F.2d 753 (7th Cir. 1948); United States v. Gasomiser Corp., 7 F.R.D. 712 (D. Del. 1947).

[31] For a valuable discussion see Spindle, *Judicial Discretion in Common Law Courts*, 4 WASH. & LEE L. REV. 143 (1947).

most—stand unappealed. As to most of his decisions he is in fact the court of last resort. This is particularly true in the local courts of criminal jurisdiction. It is the judges of these courts, moreover, especially in traffic cases, who determine, very largely by reason of the large number of people who frequent their court, the degree of public respect for the law in their community. In New Jersey last year, for example, 894,946 defendants—18.4 per cent of the population—paid their respects to the traffic courts in the aggregate sum of $5,560,509,[32] in contrast with the 191 appeals disposed of in our Supreme Court.[33]

But not all of our law by any means is judge-made. We now have a voluminous body of statutes and, over both statutes and common law, we have our written constitutions. When these statutes or constitutions become involved in litigation, the courts necessarily have to pass on their meaning in determining the case before them. Statutory construction by judges is inescapable in the administration of every system of law and is accepted everywhere, but the power of a court to declare a statute unconstitutional, involving as it does an interpretation of the constitution as well as of the statute, has been the subject of much political discussion. It is difficult to see how the courts could actually decide cases and controversies, which is their primary duty, without passing upon the question of whether a given statute falls within or without the provisions of the constitution. American courts consistently exercised these powers whenever necessary[34] even before *Marbury v. Madison*.[35] De Tocqueville sensed the implications of this inescapable judicial duty over a century ago when he said:

> "His (i.e. the American judge's) position is, therefore exactly the same as that of the magistrates of other nations; and yet he is invested with immense political power. How comes that about? . . . The cause of this difference lies in the simple fact, that the Americans have acknowledged the right of judges to found their decisions on the *Constitution* rather than on the *laws*. In other words, they have permitted them not to apply such laws as may appear to them to be unconstitutional. . . .

---

[32] Admin. Dir. of Courts Report 26 (1953-54).
[33] *The Record of the N.J. Courts in the Sixth Year Under the Constitution of 1947,* 9 RUTGERS L. REV. 489 (1955).
[34] POTTER, JUDICIAL POWER IN THE UNITED STATES 53-72 (1940). See *id.* 22-25, for instances in which colonial legislation were disapproved as contrary to English laws or colonial charters. For criticism of the doctrine of judicial review see BOUDIN, GOVERNMENT BY JUDICIARY (1932); HAINES, THE AMERICAN DOCTRINE OF JUDICIAL SUPREMACY 527-539 (2d ed. 1932). But cf. Rostow, *The Democratic Character of Judicial Review,* 66 HARV. L. REV. 193 (1952).
[35] 1 Cranch 137 (1803). In 1796 in Hylton v. United States, 3 Dallas 171, the Supreme Court had upheld the constitutionality of a federal tax statute. As Professor Beard, in THE SUPREME COURT AND THE CONSTITUTION 116 (1912) queried: "If the Court believed that it did not have the power to declare the act void as well as the power to sustain it, why did it assume jurisdiction at all or take the trouble to consider and render an opinion on the constitutionality of the tax?"

"Their power (Supreme Court justices') is enormous, but it is the power of public opinion. They are all-powerful as long as the people respect the law; but they would be impotent against popular neglect or contempt of the law. . . .

"Not only must the Federal judges be good citizens, and men of that information and integrity which are indispensable to all magistrates, but they must be statesmen, wise to discern the signs of the times, not afraid to brave the obstacles that can be subdued, nor slow to turn away from the current when it threatens to sweep them off, and the supremacy of the Union and the obedience due to the laws along with them."[36]

Admittedly the responsibility of the judge is especially momentous when it involves deciding the meaning of legislation contrary to the wishes of coordinate branches of government or of a majority of the people, but it is nonetheless one he cannot avoid. The central importance of the judges who developed the common law received a further emphasis when written constitutions were established which makes the character of those personnel who hold judicial office a matter of first interest. Today when the cumulative force of precedents, the activities of legislators and of administrative agencies leave less for judges to do in the way of developing the law to meet new situations, the decisions of judges are often of the utmost consequence because of the doctrine of judicial review.

In addition to their court duties involved in the conduct of a trial, the decision and review of a case, judges today have other duties vitally related to the proper administration of justice. These are judicial functions inherent in the tasks imposed upon the courts. Regulation of court procedure was an early manifestation of the judicial function. The earliest courts were ruled by customs developed in and by the tribunal whose activities were so governed. In the latter half of the nineteenth century after the adoption of the Field Code of Civil Procedure by New York in 1848, the legislatures of many states assumed the power to regulate judicial procedure. These statutory codes had deleterious effects, conflicting decisions interpreting them were numerous and many cases turned on procedural points rather than on the substantive issues. The American Bar Association in establishing certain minimum standards for the administration of justice recommended that "practice and procedure in the courts should be regulated by rules of court; and that to this end the courts should be given full rule making power."[37] In 1934 and 1940 the United States Supreme Court was authorized to prescribe rules of procedure for civil and criminal cases respectively in

---

[36] DEMOCRACY IN AMERICA 100, 151-152. (Reeves, text, Bowen rev. 1945).
[37] 63 A.B.A. REP. 523 (1938).

the federal courts. This power has been exercised and the success of the federal rules is the most conspicuous example of the success of a judge-made system of procedure. A definite trend towards granting the judges of the court of last resort full rule making authority over procedure has developed and today more courts are exercising this power than formerly.[38]

Judges are also entrusted with certain administrative duties which are proper concomitants of the judicial function. Every judge has responsibility for the management of his court for the most efficient conduct of its business. A system of courts in a large statewide or national organization has many of the problems inherent in the direction and management of a large business enterprise. Like a business it cannot function without proper administrative control. The proper centralization of such control naturally and logically vests in the chief justice and requires that he have the power and duty to assign judges, supervise the work of all the courts, and to call conferences of judges and others to discuss the improvement of the work of the judicial establishment. Clearly most judges have functions other than those of sitting on the bench, presiding at the trial, hearing and deciding the argument of a case, and the nonperformance of these other tasks may cause an obstruction of justice.[39]

In addition to these judicial tasks throughout the centuries judges have been entrusted with other governmental assignments. Historically this is clearly seen in the activities of the early common law judges as statesmen and advisers to the King, and in the participation of the Lord Chancellor to this day in the English cabinet. In early America this pattern was duplicated; Chief Justice Jay of the Supreme Court was called upon by President Washington to act as Ambassador to England to conduct the negotiation of a treaty with that country. In more recent years when impartiality and independence of party was required Justice Roberts headed the Pearl Harbor Commission and Justice Jackson served as the American Prosecutor of the Nazis at Nuremberg.[40] Such tasks are not properly a part of the judicial function and may even be said to derogate from the judge's proper performance of his duties. Chief Justice Stone has said:

> "A judge, and especially the Chief Justice, cannot engage in political debate or make public defense of his acts. When his action is judicial he may always rely upon the support of the defined record upon which his action is based and of the opinion in which he and

---

[38] VANDERBILT, *op. cit. supra* n. 20, at 91-145 (1949).
[39] For details of state and federal practice see *id.* at 29-90.
[40] For details see Mason, *Extra Judicial Work for Judges. The Views of Chief Justice Stone,* 67 HARV. L. REV. 193 (1953).

his associates unite as stating the ground of the decision. But where he participates in the action of the executive or legislative departments of government he is without those supports. He exposes himself to attack and indeed invites it, which because of his peculiar situation inevitably impairs his value as a judge and the appropriate influence of his office."[41]

### 3. The Rule of Law and the Development of the Anglo-American Judicial Office

Having described the proper functions of the judges, we should next consider the basic legal philosophy of the judicial office in Anglo-American law as distinguished from the civil law of Europe if we would understand their place in the social order. The underlying concept of the public law of the civilians was drawn from the Code of Justinian:

"The will of the emperor has also the force of law; since by the *lex regis* passed to define his authority, the people have granted for him and to him all their authority and power."[42]

This maxim spells absolute dictatorship,[43] whether it is of one man or of a legislative majority with the result, as Dean Pound says, "In the Roman empire and in the tradition of the civil law the judge is a part of the administrative hierarchy."[44] Thus continental judges are civil servants making a career of governmental service, securing their original appointments from and being dependent for promotions on the Ministry of Justice. While these judges dispense in many ways a high quality of justice, the entire conception of courts and judges under the civil law differs radically from that of the common law countries.[45]

The ideal of English law is in flat conflict with that of the civil law. It is the brightest thread running through the tapestry of the common law. It was early expressed by Bracton: "The king himself ought not to be subject to men, but to God and the law, because the law makes him king."[46] Lord Coke, "the oracle of the common law," was even more explicit:

---

[41] As quoted *id.* at 203-204.
[42] INSTITUTES 1.2.6. See for contrast between government in civil law countries and that of England, Fortescue's 15th century distinction between kings who rule regally and those who rule politically. DE LAUDIBUS LEGUM ANGLIE, c. IX at 25-27 (Chrimes ed. 1942).
[43] Amos, *Common Law and the Civil Law in the British Commonwealth of Nations,* in THE FUTURE OF THE COMMON LAW, 24, 30 (1937).
[44] *What is the Common Law,* in *id.* at 2, 15.
[45] See generally, ENSOR, COURTS AND JUDGES IN FRANCE, GERMANY AND ENGLAND (1933); Deak and Rheinstein, *The Machinery of Law Administration in France and Germany,* 84 U. PA. L. REV. 846 (1936). As to the difference in the position of the judge being the key to the difference between the common law and Roman law systems, see JACKSON, THE MACHINERY OF JUSTICE IN ENGLAND 18 (2d ed. 1953).
[46] As quoted in Holdsworth, *The Constitutional Position of the Judges,* 48 L.Q. REV. 25, 28 (1932).

"the King in his own person cannot adjudge any case, either criminal, as treason, felony, etc., or betwixt party and party, concerning his inheritance, chattels, or goods, etc., but this ought to be determined and adjudged in some court of justice, according to the law and custom of England. . ."[47]

These are key phrases in Anglo-American constitutional development. They were words it required courage to utter. Only if the king or governing power is subject to law is despotism impossible and only if the rights of king and citizen are subject to the impartial exposition of the judges may civil rights of the individual be developed and receive protection.

The doctrine of the rule of law which had its origins in these maxims stands for two things: (1) equality before the law and the equal subjection of all to the law as administered in the courts; and (2) the supremacy of law in contrast to arbitrary power as reflected in the Roman maxim. The rule of law has been attained in part by written constitutions, in part by legislation, but chiefly through the administration of justice in the courts by judges.[48]

It was one thing to announce an ideal of the rule of law,[49] however bravely, but it was quite another thing to achieve it. It was not for five centuries (until 1760) when it was enacted that a judge's term did not cease with the death of the king who appointed him,[50] that the last vestige of judicial dependence on the crown was abolished. Then and then only could it be said that the independence of the judiciary and the rule of law had been achieved in England. In the United States where the ideal of the rule of law was early recognized, judicial review of legislation on questions of constitutionality entrusts to the courts great responsibilities and powers. Without such power and courage in its exercise, however, the doctrine of the rule of law might be meaningless.

To understand fully what the maxims of Bracton and Coke meant to English judges we must sketch the history of the judicial office. The growth of the scope of the judicial office was inter-dependent with the development of the royal courts and the evolution of the legal profession. In England, at the outset, as in the countries of the continent the

---

[47] *Id.* at 29.
[48] See for interesting discussion, SHILS, *Populism and the Rule of Law*, in U. OF CHI., CONFERENCE ON JURISPRUDENCE AND POLITICS 91, April 30, 1954; Stone, *The Common Law in the United States,* in THE FUTURE OF THE COMMON LAW 120 (1937).
[49] "The Rule of law has no universal meaning, but in Britain it means at least the independence and integrity of the law courts. That Rule could end if the Bench were packed by an arbitrary Executive." Cecil Carr reviewing FRIEDMANN, LAW & SOCIAL CHANGE IN CONTEMPORARY GREAT BRITAIN, 4 STAN. L. REV. 616, 622 (1952).
[50] 1 Geo. III, c. 23.

judicial function was visualized as part of the royal prerogative of the sovereign.[51] Gradually, by reason of the pressure of other responsibilities, the king came more and more to turn his judicial duties over to judges appointed by him from among the royal clerks, who in early times were naturally men of the cloth because of their peculiar opportunities for learning. The judges' activities in time were differentiated from the other organs of royal government as they undertook the performance of their tasks by specialized procedures. At first judges were not the professional personnel known today; they were merely assisting the king who at any time might mount the bench. They held various commissions almost interchangeably in the several royal courts and only gradually came to be permanently assigned to a particular court.[52] These courts and the judges were the king's creation, their proceedings ran in his name, their judgments passed under his seal and were executed by his officers. The judges were appointed by the king, were removable at his will, their office terminated at his death, and the principal part of the emoluments of the offices were paid by him.[53] The courts gradually became separate organisms, but still they were the king's courts and the judges remained the king's appointees dependent for office on royal favor for many centuries.

In due time men who were not ecclesiastics began to appear in the royal courts, and in the latter part of Henry III's reign (1216-1272) some judges were being selected from among these professional practitioners of the law. In Edward I's reign (1272-1307) occurred England's first great scandal of corruption in the judiciary and a majority of the judges of the King's Bench and the Common Pleas were removed from office. With the continued development of the legal profession judges were appointed with greater frequency from that group rather than from the clerics of the royal household, but, clerics continued to be appointed to judicial office in the fourteenth century, when the practice of appointing professional lawyers became more common. By 1400 the serjeants at law, appointed by the crown from the legal practitioners, formed a select body from which judges were appointed. At that time the judges and serjeants formed "the highest branch of the legal profession,"[54] and the serjeants were consulted by the judges in the per-

---

[51] 3 BLACKSTONE, COMMENTARIES *24; COKE, FOURTH INSTITUTE *70.
[52] 1 HOLDSWORTH, HISTORY OF ENGLISH LAW 194-197, 204-211, 231-237 (5th ed. 1931); 2 *id.* at 226-232. As to the outstanding varied career of one royal judge see PUTNAM, THE PLACE IN LEGAL HISTORY OF SIR WILLIAM SHARESHULL 22-24, 153-156 (1950).
[53] 1 HOLDSWORTH, *op. cit. supra* n. 52 at 194-195, 252-255.
[54] 2 *id.* at 550. For details see *id.* at 226-230, 294-299, 311-319, 485-508. As to the corruption of the judiciary see Riddell, *Erring Judges of the Thirteenth Century*, 24 MICH. L. REV. 329 (1926). In the fifteenth century 58 of the 86 serjeants became judges. HASTINGS, THE COURT OF COMMON PLEAS IN FIFTEENTH CENTURY ENGLAND 60-65 (1947).

formance of their tasks. As the judges were selected from the legal profession, their duties became specialized and, except in rare instances, they ceased to be statesmen and advisers to the king. As the legal profession, the judiciary and the courts as institutions became separated from the royal household, they also became to an extent independent of the king. Although the serjeants and judges owed their appointments to the king and held office only at his pleasure the king's freedom of choice was circumscribed as it became customary to select appointees from practitioners at the bar, from what was a comparatively small self-governing, self-selected professional group. In the fourteenth and fifteenth centuries there were some notable instances of judges standing up against the king, although generally the king had a favored position when he appeared in court. In spite of this the judges in the royal courts became the great dispensers of justice especially between individuals.[55]

The medieval chancellors like the earlier common-law judges were churchmen who were also often statesmen. As the Chancery always retained its position as an executive office and became a recognized independent court at a later date than the common-law courts, so the chancellors maintained their connection with the royal household for a longer period than did the common-law judges. Sir Thomas More in 1529 was the first common lawyer to become chancellor and ecclesiastics were appointed to that position even thereafter. It was not until the latter half of the sixteenth century that the appointment of lawyers to the chancellorship became the settled practice.[56]

In the sixteenth and seventeenth centuries although the judges were appointed from the legal profession, the serjeants lost their former importance and appointment as a serjeant often became a mere formality preliminary to taking a seat on the bench. Until 1600 the judges were able to remain outside the religious and political controversies which divided the country. However, as constitutional questions increased and were brought before the courts as legal issues, the judges gradually became involved in the political strife of the seventeenth century. The judges, lawyers and courts were caught up in the vortex of the conflict between King and Parliament. Most of the judges, unlike Coke, became identified with the royal theories and power, and as adherents of the king some of them were subsequently punished when Parliament

---

[55] 2 HOLDSWORTH, *op. cit. supra* n. 52 at 557-564; 1 POLLOCK & MAITLAND, HISTORY OF ENGLISH LAW 204-205 (2d ed. 1899). See FORTESCUE, *op. cit. supra* n. 42 c. VIII at 21-23; c. L at 121-127, indicating the judges selected the serjeants, that no one could be appointed a judge unless a serjeant, and that no one would be selected as a serjeant who had not studied law for sixteen years.
[56] 5 HOLDSWORTH, *op. cit. supra* n. 52 at 218-225.

triumphed.[57] After the Restoration divisions of political opinion continued to embroil England and the royal prerogative over the judges was used to further the crown's own interests. Judicial tenure of office in this period was contingent on the agreement of judicial decisions with the views of the king, and judicial appointments were manipulated for the purpose of implementing their own policies by both Charles II[58] and James II.[59] The subserviency of many of the judges of the Restoration may be said to constitute a second major judicial scandal in English history.

The abuse by the Stuarts of the power of control over appointments and their removal of judges led directly to the provisions of the Act of Settlement of 1701 that:

> "Judges' commissions be made *quamdiu se bene gesserit* (during good behavior), and their salaries ascertained and established; but upon the address of both Houses of Parliament it may be lawful to remove them."[60]

And since then no judge has been dismissed or removed in England.[61] No longer dependent for the payment of their salaries or retention of their offices on royal will, the judges of England, holding office during good behavior, secured an independent position that made possible the impartial administration of justice. The achievement of this position for English judges had no direct effect on the American judiciary since the Act of Settlement was held to be inapplicable to the American colonies.[62] One of the grievances on which the colonists united in declaring their independence from the mother country concerned the royal

---

[57] HAYNES, SELECTION AND TENURE OF JUDGES 55-76 (1944); 5 HOLDSWORTH, *op. cit. supra* n. 52 at 340-354, 428.

[58] In contrast to James I, who dismissed very few judges and only one, Coke, for political reasons, during the Restoration, removal of judges was frequently resorted to. HAYNES, *op. cit. supra* n. 57 at 71-76; 6 HOLDSWORTH, *op. cit. supra* n. 52 at 213, 500-514. For interesting detailed account see Havighurst, *The Judiciary and Politics in the Reign of Charles II*, 66 L.Q. REV. 62, 229 (1950).

[59] See Havighurst, *James II and The Twelve Men in Scarlet*, 69 L.Q. REV. 522 (1953). "The Judiciary of James II is an essential part of the situation which ended in revolution. James II was as necessary to that revolution as was William of Orange. Without the constitutional conflicts of the Restoration there would have been no Bill of Rights. Complete subordination of law to politics had to be experienced before a reasonable balance could be struck. Absolute authority of King over judges had to be asserted before security of tenure for judges could be established by statute." *Id.* at 545-546. See also WILKINS, THE SPIRIT OF THE LEGAL PROFESSION 47-76 (1938).

[60] 12 & 13 William III c. 2 sec. 3(7) (1701). These provisions do not apply to judges of the county court. HANBURY, ENGLISH COURTS OF LAW 167 (2d ed. 1953). Nor do they apply to colonial judges in the British Empire. Terrell v. Sec. of State for the Colonies (1953) 2 Q.B. 482, 16 MODERN L. REV. 502 (1953).

[61] DENNING, THE CHANGING LAW 5 (1953).

[62] WASHBURNE, IMPERIAL CONTROL OF THE ADMINISTRATION OF JUSTICE IN THE THIRTEEN AMERICAN COLONIES 178-180 (Col. U. Studies in Hist., Econ., and Pubs. Law. vol. 105, no. 2, 1923). See n. 60 *supra* for present situation in British colonial possessions.

control of colonial judges.⁶³ In England, however, the judges and courts were free to make their decisions impartially, whether or not an agency of the crown was involved, without fear of recourse or dismissal.⁶⁴ And, as we have seen by the statute of 1 Geo. III, c. 23, it was enacted that the judges were continued in their offices during their good behavior, notwithstanding any demise of the king and their full salaries were absolutely secured to them during the continuance of their commissions. The significance of this act was correctly declared by George III. He

> "looked upon the independence and uprightness of the judges as essential to the impartial administration of justice; as one of the best securities of the rights and liberties of his subjects; and as most conducive to the honor of the crown."⁶⁵

At this moment Bracton's and Coke's ideal of a rule of law was realized. Mr. Justice Denning has summed up succinctly the attainment of the ideal of the reign of law in England:

> "The keystone of the rule of law in England has been the independence of the judges. It is the only respect in which we make any real separation of powers. There is no rigid separation between the legislative and the executive powers. . . . But the judicial power is truly separate. The judges for the last 250 years have been absolutely independent. . . . No member of the Government, no member of Parliament, and no official of any Government Department, has any right whatever to direct or to influence or to interfere with the decisions of any of the judges."⁶⁶

---

⁶³ The king "has obstructed the Administration of Justice, by refusing his assent to laws for establishing Judiciary Powers. . . . He has made Judges dependent on his will alone, for the tenure of their offices, and the amount and Payment of their Salaries." DUMBAULD, THE DECLARATION OF INDEPENDENCE AND WHAT IT MEANS TODAY 108-115 (1950). See also THE FEDERALIST No. 78 (Hamilton). It is to be noted that in the famous Zenger trial in the eighteenth century in New York one of the points raised by the defense was directed at the jurisdiction of the court and attacked the legality of the commissions of the judges conducting the trial on the ground that they were "during pleasure" and not for "good behavior". See MORRIS, FAIR TRIAL 69, 78 (1952). In New York in 1761 after judges had refused to act under commissions which did not give them tenure during good behavior, instructions were sent to colonial governors ordering judicial commissions should be made during pleasure only. Laws providing for tenure during good behavior enacted by colonial legislatures were disapproved. DUMBAULD, op. cit. supra 112-115.

⁶⁴ Thus 1 BLACKSTONE, COMMENTARIES *269: "In this distinct and separate existence of the judicial power in a peculiar body of men, nominated indeed, but not removable at pleasure, by the crown, consists one main preservative of the public liberty, which cannot subsist long in any state unless the administration of common justice be in some degree separated both from the legislative and also from the executive power. . . ."

⁶⁵ Preamble, 1 GEO. III c. 23 (1760).

⁶⁶ THE CHANGING LAW 4 (1953). See also HANBURY, op. cit. supra n. 60 at 162-169.

## 4. The Essential Characteristics of Judicial Office

In the eight centuries or more in which the judicial office has evolved in the Anglo-American system of law, three essentials stand out in any definition of a true judge. These are impartiality, independence and immunity. Of these impartiality is the most important; independence and immunity are the means of achieving impartiality. Judges should be free from every tie which may sway their judgment. They should be answerable to no one and immune from liability for judicial acts, to the end that justice may be administered without favor. The independence that judges must have to administer the law impartially was achieved only after the courts became separated from other governmental organs and only, as we have seen, when it was recognized that justice was a mockery and a farce if the judges were dependent on other departments of government for their income or for the retention of their office. Without these all the personal qualifications of the judge—his character, courage, honesty, wisdom and learning—are of little import or value save in unusual crises, where the judge is called to stand up to a test that it is not fair or wise to impose on any man.

Recognition of the indispensability and interdependency of these incidents of judicial office was slow in coming. The first royal judges and the American colonial judges were the king's creatures, appointed by him, removable at his will, and their tenure of office terminated at his death. It was only as a better brand of justice, a more just justice, was expected and demanded and when the effects of the royal pressures on the judiciary were felt by the people that the need was realized for the immunity and independence of the judiciary.

Impartiality is part of the definition of a good judge. We have sketched the historical process by which a reign of law was achieved for the citizen while at the same time making the judges independent. As long as a judge is subject to removal or the threat thereof, or to pressure, or influence, his judicial decisions obviously cannot be expected to be impartial. And so not until judges of the English courts were commissioned to hold office during good behavior, with certain compensation, may they be said to have achieved those measures necessary to the independence that make for impartiality.[67] Quite as important as the effect of these statutes on the judiciary was their effect on litigants and the public. With their passage any doubt that they might have entertained as to the independence in fact of judges from governmental pressure was entirely dissipated. As Chief Judge John J. Parker well put it:

---

[67] "The judge is independent in a sense which is no doubt of vital importance; but that independence, in its turn, is so subtly related to the problem of impartiality as to make the latter the real clue to what independence implies."

"a judge must not only be independent—absolutely free of all influence and control so that he can put into his judgments the honest, unfettered and unbiased judgment of his mind, but he must be so freed of business, political and financial connections and obligations that the public will recognize that he is independent."[68]

We have been discussing the independence necessary to the judicial office without which the independent individual cannot function freely and impartially, but there is another kind of independence and impartiality that is equally important—that relates to the character of the judge himself. He must be able to think things through for himself and not be so easily swayed by arguments on one side as to cause him to close his mind to the other side of the case. He must be independent in mind so as to evaluate both precedents and contemporary needs, to balance them and, fearless of public opinion, to render impartial judgment. He must be independent in the sense that he is self-reliant and not submissive, able to make decisions freely without being subject to bias and influence. This is a matter of individual personality; it is independence in the sense of the courageous character of a particular person. It is quite as important as the independence that is accorded any constitution or statute. But it can only be obtained through the proper selection of judges.

Judicial independence has been enhanced by the development of the common-law doctrine of judicial immunity that has enabled judges to be free from fear of recrimination for the consequences of their judicial decisions. Gradually it became a principle of English law that judges were not liable civilly for judicial acts within their jurisdiction. This doctrine was clearly recognized by the seventeenth century[69] and has been applied without exception since then. The doctrine of immunity protects the Anglo-American judge when acting in his judicial capacity so that he may be independent in his decisions, although when he does perform actions not strictly required as part of his judicial function, he may be legally liable.[70]

---

"Impartiality, clearly, has two sides. On the one hand it means a willingness to allow all to be said in Court that relevance and the rules of evidence permit: to be said, moreover, in such a way that it is able to carry its full weight. On the other, it means an ability to bring to the task of decision a mind that can rise above all considerations of personal conviction and private feeling." Laski, *supra* n. 1 at 115, 121.

[68] *The Judicial Office in the United States*, 23 N.Y.U.L. REV. 225, 228 (1948).

[69] See HOLDSWORTH, *Immunity for Judicial Acts*, 1924 J. SOC. PUB. TEACHERS OF LAW 17.

[70] For the historical origins of the doctrine see Yates v. Lansing, 5 Johns 282 (N.Y. 1810). In Bradley v. Fisher, 80 U.S. (13 Wall.) 335 Mr. Justice Field in holding a judge was not liable in a civil action if the complaint concerned a judicial act stated: "Liability to answer to everyone who might feel himself aggrieved by the action of the judge, would be inconsistent with the possession of this freedom (of judges to act without fear of personal consequences), and would

## 5. Tenure of Judicial Office and an Independent Judiciary

The early experience with judges in the American settlements paralleled that of the English. One of the complaints of the American colonists was directed at the fact that the English Act of Settlement of 1701 was held not to extend to the colonies,[71] and that consequently colonial judges held office merely at the pleasure of the crown.[72] The Declaration of Independence reflected colonial recognition of the importance of an independent judiciary and of the fact that such independence was in no small way based on tenure during good behavior:

> "He (George III) has made judges dependent on his will alone, for the tenure of their offices, and the amount and payment of their salaries."

Since one of the colonial complaints was directed at the uncertain tenure of their judges and their subserviency to the crown it was only natural that representatives of the thirteen sovereign states would desire an independent judiciary for their union, a judiciary subject to no factional pressures or influences of the legislature or executive, which one or the other groups of states might dominate.[73] Under this new federal system the need for an independent judiciary secure in their tenure seemed self-evident, if the elaborate scheme of checks and balances was to function properly.[74] In the making of the federal constitution the question of

---

destroy that independence without which no judiciary can be either respectable or useful" (at 347). As to limits of judicial immunity, see Murray v. Brancato, 290 N.Y. 52, 48 N.E.2d 257 (1943).

[71] See n. 62 *supra.*

[72] See n. 63 *supra.* See WASHBURNE, *op. cit. supra* n. 62 at 178-180, for instances when the colonies tried to provide for tenure during good behavior. The colonists in contending with the crown argued that tenure during the pleasure of the king led to subserviency of judges and tolerance of arbitrary actions of the executive, but the crown considered that because of the scarcity of available personnel often it had to appoint men who were not particularly competent and it did not want to have to retain them when more qualified personnel appeared. In 1761 the Board of Trade noted that a policy of appointment during good behavior would be "subversive of all true policy, destructive to the interests of Your Majesty's subjects and tending to lessen that just dependence which the colonies ought to have upon the government of the mother country." *Id.* at 180.

[73] The Federalist, No. 78 at 528 (Ford ed. 1898): "That inflexible and uniform adherence to the rights of the Constitution, and of individuals, which we perceive to be indispensable in the courts of justice, can certainly not be expected from judges who hold their offices by a temporary commission. Periodical appointments, however regulated, or by whomsoever made, would, in some way or other, be fatal to their necessary independence. If the power of making them was committed either to the executive or legislature, there would be danger of an improper complaisance to the branch which possessed it: if to both, there would be unwillingness to hazard the displeasure of either; if to the people, or to persons chosen by them for the special purpose, there would be too great a disposition to consult popularity, and to justify a reliance that nothing would be consulted but the Constitution and the laws."

[74] Thus the rejection of the suggestion that the judges be constituted a Council of Revision to join in approval of statutes. 2 FARRAND, RECORDS OF THE FEDERAL CONVENTION 73-80 (1923).

tenure during good behavior was hardly a question for debate, since all four of the principal plans submitted to the Convention had such a provision.[75]

From the first the federal government[76] and a majority of the original states provided tenure during good behavior for their judiciary. These officials had a lifetime office subject only in most jurisdictions to impeachment in cases of improper behavior.[77] A majority of the new states admitted before 1830 also provided for life tenure for the judiciary.[78] For several decades it was generally accepted, as the provisions embodied in the federal constitution and a majority of the early state constitutions bear witness, that tenure in office during good behavior was essential to an independent judiciary subservient to no persons or bodies, subject to no pressures or influences.[79] This view is most vividly expressed in the Massachusetts Constitution of 1780:

"It is essential to the preservation of the rights of every individual, his life, liberty, property, and character, that there be an impartial interpretation of the laws, and administration of justice. It is the right of every citizen to be tried by judges as free, impartial and

---

[75] Virginia (Randolph), 1 *id.* 20, 21 Resolution 9; New Jersey (Paterson) *id.* 242, 244 (Proposition 5); South Carolina (Pinckney) 3 *id.*, Appendix D, 595, 600 (Art. 9); Hamilton, 1 *id.* 292 (VII); see also 3 *id.* 617, 625 (Art. V). Thomas Jefferson, who later was bitterly critical of the lifetime federal judiciary, in 1776 agreed that judges "should not be dependent upon any man or body of men. To these ends they should hold estates for life. . . . Their commissions should be during good behavior." IV WRITINGS 259 (Library ed. 1904).

[76] U.S. CONST. ART. III, sec. 1: ". . . The Judges, both of the Supreme and Inferior Courts, shall hold their offices during good behavior, and shall, at stated times, receive for their services, a compensation, which shall not be diminished during their continuance in office."

[77] Del., Md., Mass., N.H., N.Y., N.C., S.C., and Va. CARPENTER, JUDICIAL TENURE IN THE UNITED STATES 4 (1918). In New York a mandatory retirement age of 60 was fixed. In Connecticut and Rhode Island judges' continuance in office was originally dependent on the annual action of the legislature. In Georgia probably this was the original practice but in 1789 judges were accorded three year terms. In New Jersey Supreme Court judges had seven year terms and other judges five years. In Pennsylvania seven year terms were accorded judges initially but in 1790 tenure during good behavior was provided. For summary of relevant provisions and later changes see *id.* 101 *et seq.*; HAYNES, *op. cit. supra* n. 57 at 101-135.

[78] Eight of the eleven states: Ala., Ill., Ky., La., Me., Miss., Mo., and Tenn. Haynes, Selection and Tenure of Judges 99-101, 110-118, 130 (1944). The three which provided for terms of years were Indiana, Ohio and Vermont.

[79] It is only recently with the establishment of the Administrative Office of the Courts that the federal judiciary have achieved the ultimate in independence of the executive to whom formerly they had to look for many matters connected with the management of the business of the courts. And, of course, as long as the power of the purse belongs to Congress, that body has a theoretical measure of control of the courts, though it is not to be imagined that Congress would so abuse this power as to bring pressure on the judiciary through this means. The British manage this problem by making judicial salaries a charge on the Consolidated Fund, securing the payment even if Parliament does not meet and judicial salaries do not have to be authorized annually. JACKSON, MACHINERY OF JUSTICE 224-225 (2d ed. 1953).

independent as the lot of humanity will admit. It is, therefore, not only the best policy, but for the security of the rights of the people, and of every citizen, that the judges of the supreme judicial court should hold their offices as long as they behave themselves well; and that they should have honorable salaries ascertained and established by standing laws."[80]

When at various times the Supreme Court of the United States has for one reason or another been caught up in the maelstrom of politics and limited terms of office for the federal judiciary have been proposed,[81] none of these have been successful and judges of the federal constitutional courts have retained tenure during good behavior.[82] Gradually in the early nineteenth century, however, as a reaction to the growth and extension of judicial activity and the seeming thwarting of the popular will by court decisions, fear of the power of the judges developed among some sections of public opinion.[83] A belief grew that judicial independence and lack of responsibility to the people were dangerous and undemocratic.[84] Those who defended life tenure argued as did Chief Justice Marshall:

> "The independence of all those who try causes between man and man, and between a man and his Government, can be maintained only by the tenure of their office . . . if they may be removed at pleasure, will any lawyer of distinction come upon your bench?

---

[80] Part I, Art. xxix.

[81] *E.g.* BROOKS, WALTER CLARK, FIGHTING JUDGE 193-196 (1944); 1 WARREN, SUPREME COURT IN UNITED STATES HISTORY 313 (rev. ed. 1947).

[82] The constitutional guarantees of tenure during good behavior do not, however, extend to judges of the legislative and territorial courts, although such tenure has been accorded to some of these judges by Congress. See Brown, *The Rent in Our Judicial Armor*, 10 GEO. WASH. L. REV. 127 (1941), adverting to the danger that litigants suing the federal government in federal courts may "at the whim of Congress, be deprived of the protection of an independent court to determine their controversies" at 129. The legislative courts are the Court of Claims, the Customs Court and the Court of Customs and Patent Appeals, the judges of which now have been accorded life tenure by Congress (28 U.S.C.A. sec. 173, 213, 252) but this tenure is dependent on congressional will. Judges of the district courts in Hawaii and Puerto Rico do not have life tenure (28 U.S.C.A. sec. 134). When the Judiciary Act of 1801 was repealed, one of the questions which was much debated was that of the tenure of office of Federalist appointees under that statute when the offices were abolished. BEVERIDGE, III LIFE OF JOHN MARSHALL 58-96 (1919); CARPENTER, *op. cit. supra* n. 77, at 60-78 (1912). Congress decided that the abolition of the courts to which the judges were appointed resulted in the abolition of their right to judicial office, but no judicial review of this question was ever obtained. 1 WARREN, *op. cit. supra* n. 81, at 193, 206-214.

[83] See CARPENTER, *op. cit. supra* n. 77, 168-176.

[84] In a letter written in 1822 Thomas Jefferson said: "Let the future appointments of judges be for four or six years, and renewable by the President and Senate. This will bring their conduct, at regular intervals under revision and probation. . . . We have erred in this point, by copying England, where certainly it is a good thing to have judges independent of the King. . . . That there should be public functionaries independent of the nation, whatever may be their merit, is a solicism in a republic, of the first order of absurdity and inconsistency." JEFFERSON, XV WORKS 389 (Library ed. 1904).

No Sir. I have always thought, from my earliest youth till now, that the greatest scourge an angry Heaven ever inflicted upon an ungrateful and sinning people, was an ignorant, a corrupt, or a dependent Judiciary."[85]

Although attacks on the tenure of the federal judiciary were generally unsuccessful,[86] the imposition of limits on the tenure of those in state judicial office usually accompanied and even preceded the democratically inspired alterations in the manner of selection for that office[87] and was part of the effort to make the judiciary more responsive to the people.

Today judges hold office during good behavior only in the federal courts, Massachusetts and New Hampshire. In New Jersey, following their reappointment after an initial seven year term, the judges of the Supreme and Superior Courts have life tenure, subject to retirement at the age of 70. Interestingly enough in Rhode Island judges of the superior court (the general trial court) who are appointed by the governor hold office for life, while the judges of the Supreme Court who are elected by the legislature hold office subject to the right of the legislature to declare the office vacant.[88] In the other states varying terms of

---

[85] PROCEEDINGS AND DEBATES OF THE VIRGINIA CONVENTION OF 1829-1830, 619 (1830). Chief Justice Marshall also said: "The argument of the gentlemen goes to prove not only that there is no such thing as Judicial Independence, but that there ought to be no such thing: that it is unwise and improvident to make the tenure of the Judge's office to continue during good behavior. . . . I have grown old in the opinion that there is nothing more dear to Virginia, or ought to be dearer to her statesmen, and that the best interests of our country are secured by it. Advert, Sir, to the duties of a Judge. He has to pass between the government and the man whom the court is prosecuting; between the most powerful individual in the community, and the poorest and most unpopular. . . . The Judicial Department comes home in its effects to every man's fireside; it passes on his property, his reputation, his life, his all. Is it not to the last degree important, that he should be rendered perfectly and completely independent, with nothing to influence or control him but God and his conscience. You do not allow a man to perform the duties of a juryman or a Judge, if he has one dollar of interest in the matter to be decided; and will you allow a Judge to give a decision when his office may depend upon it? When his decision may offend a powerful and influential man? . . . I acknowledge that, in my judgment, the whole good which may grow out of this Convention . . . will never compensate for the evil of changing the tenure of the Judicial office." *Id.* at 616.

[86] HAINES, ROLE OF OUR SUPREME COURT IN AMERICAN GOVERNMENT AND POLITICS 259-265 (1944), discusses the Jeffersonian attempt to use the impeachment device to control the judiciary. See also CARPENTER, *op. cit. supra* n. 77 at 109 *et seq.*; Burton, *An Independent Judiciary: The Keystone of Our Freedom*, 39 A.B.A.J. 1067 (1953).

[87] Between 1830 and the Civil War the tenure of judges was limited in 21 states. CARPENTER, *op. cit. supra* n. 77 at 176-179. Since 1846 every state which has been admitted has provided for popular election of judges for a term of years. HAYNES, *op. cit. supra* n. 57 at 100. As early as 1816 Indiana's original constitution provided that judges who were appointed by the governor were to have seven-year terms. Louisiana in 1845 retained appointment by the governor but limited judicial tenure to 8 years. Missouri in 1848 likewise retained gubernatorial appointment but adopted a limited tenure. *Id.* 110, 113, 118.

[88] VANDERBILT, *op. cit. supra* n. 20, at 17; In 1953 a proposed amendment to R.I. CONST., ART. X, 54 providing for judicial tenure during good behavior or until a judge has attained 70 years and had 15 years of service approved by the

years are provided, ranging from as little as two years in Vermont to 21 years for Supreme Court Justices in Pennsylvania. In the majority of states in which judges are elected the term of office of both trial and appellate judges varies from five to ten years. In those states where judges are customarily retained in office and in those in which the terms of office are more than ten years, tenure in some respects approximates tenure during good behavior until the age of retirement[89] is reached subject always to the political uncertainties of partisan defeat when one party sweeps an election on national issues. As one western judge wittily put it, he was elected by Wilson and defeated by Harding.

The problem of the tenure to be given judges is inextricably interrelated with the question of the degree of independence necessary for the fulfillment of judicial functions.[90] To a public for whom equality is a by-word lengthy terms of office or tenure during good behavior may

---

legislature was rejected by the electorate in November, 1954. R.I. Acts, c. 3096 (1953); ELLIOTT, *Judicial Administration,* 30 N.Y.U.L. REV. 966, 969 (1955). As recently as 1935 the Rhode Island Legislature declared the offices of the Supreme Court judges vacant and removed all the sitting justices who had from five to twenty years of service on the bench. For details of this partisan action see *Recent Legislative Election of Supreme Court Justice in Rhode Island,* 21 A.B.A.J. 306 (1935).

[89] VANDERBILT, *op. cit. supra* n. 20, at 17-20; 1954-1955 BOOK OF THE STATES 435. States in which there are terms of more than 10 years for all or some judges are: Calif., Colo., Del., La., Md., Mo., N.Y., N.D., Pa., S. Car., Utah, Va., W. Va., and Wisconsin. Another limitation on tenure which must be mentioned is that which establishes an age limit for those holding judicial office. Where such is the case and judges must vacate their office at a certain age their tenure of office is accordingly limited, but not rendered insecure. The question of age is vital in considering the tenure to be accorded judges since when judges hold office during good behavior and no retiring age is obligatory the public may be burdened with judges who are unable to properly discharge the duties of their office and yet remain on the bench. See Fairman, *The Retirement of Federal Judges,* 51 HARV. L. REV. 397 (1938), discussing various aspects of compulsory retirement for judges. "The sound argument for a retiring age is that judges must inspire confidence, and that on the whole people do not care to be judged by those who belong to a generation that is generally inactive." JACKSON, *op. cit. supra* n. 79 at 230. But cf. statement of CHIEF JUSTICE HUGHES, THE SUPREME COURT OF THE UNITED STATES 74-75 (1928): "The community has no more valuable asset than an experienced judge. . . . Doubtless there is a time when a judge reaches, on account of age, the limit of effective service, but it is very difficult to fix that time." A constitutional amendment to require federal judges to retire at 75 has been proposed. 40 J. AM. JUD. SOC'Y 23 (1951). Obligatory retirement at a certain age is not commonly mandatory in the United States, although permissible retirement with pension arrangements is authorized in most states in order to encourage the resignation from office of those who are no longer capable of performing their duties by making financial arrangements for their continued support. 1954-1955 BOOK OF THE STATES 440-441. For history of practices as to retirement see CARPENTER, *op. cit. supra* n. 77, at 186-192.

[90] Thus the observations of two noted English students of these matters: "an insecure judiciary tends inevitably to corruption." Laski, *Procedure for Constructive Contempt in England,* 41 HARV. L. REV. 1031 (1928); "The security of tenure . . . is founded on the belief that a man cannot be relied upon to act rightly regardless of the personal consequences." ROBSON, JUSTICE AND ADMINISTRATIVE LAW 44, 45 (2d ed. 1947).

seem aristocratic.[91] The popular feeling that all can equally administer justice and that experience in these tasks is of little importance makes it difficult for the public to realize the value of continuity in judicial office. It is too often forgotten that the judicial task is a specialized one. Historically short terms of office have gone hand in hand with the selection of judges by the electorate. This may be explained as the result of the democratic fervor which swept the country a century or more ago. Limitations on judicial tenure and popular election of judges were the first expedients of a people critical of their courts and desirous of influencing and controlling judicial decisions. Because of the manifold difficulties in selecting those fit for such specialized tasks short terms may be used as a device to check the abuse of the office by those temporarily placed there and as a means of removal of those unfit for office, but without any assurance that the replacements will be any better than those whom they replace. Unless tenure is secure it is difficult to attract the ablest men to the bench or for them to develop their abilities to administer justice impartially. The judicial task differs so greatly from the work of advocacy at the bar that it is difficult for a new judge to perfect himself in the judicial job of impartiality without reasonable tenure. Moreover, under a system of short terms of office, tenure may not depend on the judge's performance, but on the turn of the wheel of fortune at the polls, something quite beyond his individual control when one party sweeps into office by such an overwhelming vote that all other officeholders of the other party, no matter how valuable their work may have been, are turned out of office by an electorate voting a straight ticket.[92] The judiciary should be as free from problems in their selection as in the performance of their judicial tasks.

## II

### THE ATTRIBUTES AND THE SELECTION OF JUDGES

#### 1. *Attributes of a Good Judge*

Every writer on the subject of judges comes up with his own list of the essential attributes of a good judge. These lists naturally vary according to the experience of each writer. An English writer would be less likely, for example, to stress professional competence than an American writer. English judges are appointed by the crown on the recommendation in most instances of the Lord Chancellor from among the barristers of at least ten years' standing with respect to the High

---

[91] Cf. CHOATE'S COMMENTS TO THE MASSACHUSETTS CONSTITUTIONAL CONVENTION OF 1853, reprinted in 17 J. AM. JUD. SOC'Y 10, 12-13 (1936). See also 2 STORY, COMMENTARIES ON THE CONSTITUTION, sec. 1621 (4th ed., Cooley, 1873).

[92] See Lecture II *infra* and quotation from N.Y. Times of Nov. 4, 1954, at n. 60.

Court and seven years in the case of the County Courts. The rest—a group of higher judges—are appointed by the crown on the recommendation of the Prime Minister, who, however, consults the Lord Chancellor as to his selections. These judges must be barristers of at least fifteen years' standing. By Magna Carta King John covenanted that "justices . . . shall be appointed such as know the law and mean duly to observe it."[1] Accordingly, the professional competency of an English judge is taken for granted.

In the early years in this country, on the other hand, little attention was paid to the requirements with respect to professional competence. Many members of the bar and indeed many judges had little or no legal learning,[2] and few requirements of any sort were made of the pioneer judges.[3] Today many states do require that judges be qualified in

---

[1] MAGNA CARTA, c. 45. TASWELL-LANGMEAD, ENGLISH CONSTITUTIONAL HISTORY 88 (10th ed. Plucknett, 1946).

[2] In the colonies after independent courts supplanted the legislature and when there were few lawyers available, of necessity the judges were usually laymen with the possible exception of the chief justice. A tradition of lay service on the bench was developed and it was not until the Revolution that it was considered desirable or necessary to have learned judges. AUMANN, THE CHANGING AMERICAN LEGAL SYSTEM: SOME SELECTED PHASES 34-42 (1940).

It has been pointed out, however, that "It is a mistake to assume that other (lay) members of the highest judicial tribunal of the province (Mass.) were not familiar with the legal learning of the times because not educated for or trained by practice in the legal profession" and that "It is not probable that so far as familiarity with books of law could give equipment for judicial work, the trained lawyers of the court were so much better furnished than their associates as might be hastily assumed." Mason, *Short History of the Supreme Court of Massachusetts Prior to 1780*, 2 MASS. L.Q. 82, 97 (1916).

Of the first judges of the Illinois Supreme Court, one was never a lawyer, another who had no legal training had been a district attorney and sat on the Supreme Court for thirty years. King, *A Pioneer Court of Last Resort*, 20 ILL. L. REV. 573 (1936). In New Jersey in 1777, two of the Supreme Court justices were not lawyers. Of the three justices of the New Hampshire Superior Court appointed after the Revolution was a theologian, another a physician. A judge of the highest court of Rhode Island in 1814-1818 was a blacksmith, and a farmer was chief justice there from 1819 to 1826. POUND, THE LAWYER FROM ANTIQUITY TO MODERN TIMES 179 (1953) n. 4. See also Corning, *The Highest Courts of New Hampshire*, 2 G.B. 469, 470 (1890) as to legal learning not being requisite for judges until long after the Revolution; Whitehead, *Supreme Court of New Jersey*, 3 G.B. 355, 366 (1891). The second chief justice of Vermont also was a physician. Taft, *Supreme Court of Vermont*, 6 G.B. 16, 18, 72, 122 (1894). The first Vermont judge with a legal education was Nathanial Chipman, who served on the bench with four laymen in 1786. *Id*. at 24. See *id*. at 75 as to Theophilus Harrington, who was a judge of the Supreme Court for ten years though not admitted to the bar until after his first election as Supreme Court judge and whose successive reelections indicated the satisfaction with which his work was received. Harrington, it was reported, having heard two leading lawyers argue a question under a demurrer, "listened attentively for a long time, then taking the demurrer in his hand said, 'Mr. Chipman, what do you call that?' 'That is a demurrer, Your Honor.' Turning to Mr. Smith, he said, 'Do you call it a demurrer?' He answered in the affirmative; whereupon Judge Harrington said, 'I do not know as the court knows what a demurrer is, but it knows what justice is, and this plaintiff is entitled to a judgment.'" *Id*. at 76.

[3] See n. 2 *supra* for details. On the western frontier it was often necessary to rely on the justice of the peace for local dispensation of justice because of the

law and that they have legal experience.⁴ "At best these are minimum qualifications and give small inkling of how learned it is necessary for a judge to be. . . . While we may assume that some knowledge of the law is a necessary part of a judge's equipment, it does not follow that any given level of legal training or knowledge should be required of all judges on any given court."⁵ In this country where so many of our judges are elected to office in popularity contests and so many even of those who are appointed are selected with political considerations in mind, professional competence cannot be taken for granted and hence considerable attention is devoted here to the need of professional training and experience.

The attributes of a good judge are epitomized in the Canons of Judicial Ethics formulated by a committee of outstanding leaders of the American Bar headed by William Howard Taft and adopted by the American Bar Association.⁶ These canons, which incorporate the traditional standards set up for sound judicial behavior, have been either expressly adopted or they are tacitly accepted in most of the states. The Canons of Judicial Ethics are too long to quote in full, but we may cull from the canons a brief statement of a judge's conduct:

> ". . . Every judge should at all times be alert in his rulings and in the conduct of the business of the court, so far as he can, to make

---

frontier conditions of isolation and lawlessness. These lay justices were singularly undistinguished for the way in which they filled judicial office. GARD, FRONTIER JUSTICE (1949) gives some interesting examples of their activities. At 254-270. Mary Williams in her HISTORY OF THE SAN FRANCISCO COMMITTEE OF VIGILANCE OF 1851 (1921) reports that a traveller in a remote district of California wrote in 1852: One of the judges of this court is at the same time a justice of the peace, sign painter, postmaster, miner, engineer, carpenter, doctor, boarding house keeper, and assistant surveyor of the district—having thus ten independent functions, all of which he fills with credit to himself and advantage to the community. You will often find a man on the bench one year, and in the middle of the river the next. See also Nerinck, *Legal Life in the American Far-West*, 14 YALE L.J. 380 (1905).

⁴ In 32 states the trial judges and in 23 states the appellate judges must be learned in law, while legal experience is required of appellate judges in 28 states and of trial court judges in 30 states. 1954-1955 BOOK OF THE STATES 437. Even without such prescriptions judges of the appellate courts and trial courts of general jurisdiction are commonly lawyers. In Michigan, where there are no statutory professional qualifications for judges of the Circuit Court, all present judges have been admitted to the bar. VIRTUE, SURVEY OF METROPOLITAN COURTS, DETROIT AREA 56-59 (1950).

It is to be noted that requirements of legal learning and legal experience embody no definite standards. Even where a judge is required to be "learned in the law", it has been held that such a requirement is merely a direction to the voters and does not necessarily mean that the judge be a licensed attorney. Heard v. Moore, 154 Tenn. 566, 290 S.W. 15 (1926). But cf. decisions to the contrary cited in Jamieson v. Wiggin, 12 S.D. 16, 80 N.W. 137 (1899), which was followed by State ex rel. Jack v. Schmal, 125 Minn. 533, 147 N.W. 425 (1914).

⁵ Mott, *Measurement of Judicial Personnel*, 23 N.Y.U.L.Q. REV. 262, 271-272 (1946).

⁶ The first 34 canons were adopted in 1924. Canons 35 and 36 were adopted in 1937, and Canons 28, 30 and 35 have been amended. DRINKER, LEGAL ETHICS 274 (1953).

it useful to litigants and to the community. He should avoid unconsciously falling into the attitude of mind that litigants are made for the courts instead of the courts for the litigants. . . . A judge's official conduct should be free from impropriety and the appearance of impropriety; . . . his personal behavior, . . . should be beyond reproach. . . . A judge should be temperate, attentive, patient, impartial, and, . . . he should be studious of the principles of the law and diligent in endeavoring to ascertain the facts. . . . A judge should exhibit an industry and application commensurate with the duties imposed upon him. . . . A judge should be prompt in the performance of his judicial duties. . . . A judge should be considerate of jurors, witnesses and others in attendance upon the court. . . . A judge should be courteous to counsel. . . . The power of making . . . appointments should not be exercised by him for personal or partisan advantage. . . . A judge should not be swayed by partisan demands, public clamor or considerations of personal popularity or notoriety, nor be apprehensive of unjust criticism. . . . In every particular his conduct should be above reproach. He should be conscientious, studious, thorough, courteous, patient, punctual, just, impartial, fearless of public clamor, regardless of public praise, and indifferent to private political or partisan influences; he should administer justice according to law, and deal with his appointments as a public trust; he should not allow other affairs or his private interests to interfere with the prompt and proper performance of his judicial duties nor should he administer the office for the purpose of advancing his personal ambitions or increasing his popularity."[7]

From this summary of the duties of judges and from studies that have been made of those who have held judicial office,[8] the chief attributes necessary for such work may be readily identified.[9] For every

---

[7] Canons 2, 4, 5, 6, 7, 9, 10, 12, 14, 34. As set out *id.* at 328-337. The various canons incorporate many admonitions as to judicial behavior which indicate the scope and limit of judicial activity. See in particular Canons 3, 8, 11, 12, 15-23. Canons 13, 24-33 are recommendations as to what judges should not do. These standards are not new. In the 13th century Bracton wrote:

"Let not one, who is unwise and unlearned, ascend the judgment seat, which is, as it were, the throne of God. . . . And when a person is obliged to judge and to be a judge, let him take care of himself, lest by judging perversely and against the laws, through entreaties or for a price, for the advantage of a paltry temporary gain, he presumes to bring upon himself the sadness of external grief. . . .

"A judge ought not only to be wise, but powerful, according to the saying of Solomon. Avoid seeking to be a judge, unless thou art strong in virtue to break through iniquities, lest by chance thou shouldst fear the face of the powerful man, and cause scandal. . . ." LAWS AND CUSTOMS OF ENGLAND Vol. I, 9; Vol. II, 181 (Twiss ed. Rolls ser. No. 70, 1878).

[8] See among others, EWING, THE JUDGES OF THE SUPREME COURT, 1789-1937 (1938); MARTIN, THE ROLE OF THE BAR IN ELECTING THE BENCH IN CHICAGO (1936); Hoopes, *An Experiment in the Measurement of Judicial Qualifications in the Supreme Court of Ohio*, 18 U. CIN. L. REV. 417 (1949); Mott, Albright & Semmerling, *Judicial Personnel*, 167 ANNALS 143 (1933); Mott, *Measurement of Judicial Personnel*, 23 N.Y.U.L. REV. 262 (1948); Neitzert, *Judges of Nisi Prius Courts of Illinois*, 30 ILL. L. REV. 469 (1935).

[9] Cf. LUMMUS, THE TRIAL JUDGE, 15-25 (1937); the *Table of Qualities Desirable in a Judge*, Martin, *op. cit. supra* n. 8 at ·122; Jenkyn, *Improvements to*

judge we may establish certain requirements as to character, intellect, knowledge, and human relations. The requirement of integrity of character is primary; in order for judges to be independent and impartial they must be courageous and able to withstand external influences whether in the form of bribes, pressure of friend or family, antipathies of class or religion. The importance of the ethics of a judge cannot be overemphasized. Judges require that true humility of character that is found in an awareness of one's own limitations and deficiencies and finds expression in a willingness to hear the other side of the question.[10] Wisdom, that deepening of the intellect which is more than mere intelligence, including comprehension of the effects of their decisions, is fundamental if a judge is to be able to resolve all the ramifications of the various kinds of litigation coming before him. Knowledge in the fullest sense of learning and education, legal and general, and professional experience, are the handmaidens of such wisdom. Social relations embrace personal conduct, the maturity which comes with experience of people, the ability to get along with other men, to understand their actions[11] and to decide in accordance with such understanding, and to evoke the respect of other men by attitudes of courtesy and cooperation. A judge does not function in the isolation of an ivory tower; he must deal with the disputes of actual people and he must know and understand them. The trial judge is in some ways a solitary figure, but in his relations with litigants, witnesses, lawyers, the court staffs and the public he must reveal a knowledge of human nature or he will not be able to fulfill his tasks. Understanding people and the inner motives that inspire their actions is equally important to the trial and the appellate judge. The appellate judge, who has little intercourse with litigants and witnesses, must be able to understand them with even less contact than the trial judge and he must be able to act in cooperation with his associates on the bench and counsel before him, if the court is to accomplish its work satisfactorily.[12] Relatively few judges have all these qualifications, and

---

the *Judicial System*, 27 AUSTR. L.J. 145 (1953); Parker, *The Judicial Office in the United States*, 23 N.Y.U.L.Q. REV. 225, 227-229 (1948).

[10] "Men ask more than scholarship, however, of a judge, and in this they are right, for while scholarship may clear the thickets it can build little. In the end, and quite fairly, a judge will be estimated in terms of his outlook and his nature. He cannot evade responsibility for his beliefs, because these are at bottom the creatures of his choice . . . the wise man is the detached man." HAND, SPIRIT OF LIBERTY 27, 132 (2d ed. Dilliard 1953).

[11] Cf. BOK, BACKBONE OF THE HERRING 146 (1941); "For one of his (the judge's) cases that was ruled by a pure point of law there were ten that were determined by the behavior and personality of the litigants."

[12] "The judges of a supreme court are not only the central figures in the court room; they are almost the sole figures. . . . A frank judge can recount case after case which was determined by the discussion among the judges in conferences, rather than by lawyers' arguments or even the briefs." Mott, Albright & Semmerling, *Judicial Personnel*, 167 ANNALS 143 (1933). But cf. as to the danger

yet which of these attributes can be deemed superfluous?

The attributes we have been discussing are basic and yet except for those relating to education and legal training it would seem to be impossible to formulate standards for their attainment which are external and objective. Even the extent of education that is requisite may be incapable of definition. Is education in a law school essential? Or will education in a good law office suffice? Or is a combination of the two to be preferred? And study of what subjects will best prepare one for judicial office? Is legal learning sufficient or is education in economics, government, sociology, ethics, history, the arts and the sciences also essential for the "compleat" judge?

The requirement of legal experience is also fraught with ambiguities. What kind of legal experience is desirable? Some of the greatest United States Supreme Court justices have been those who never had prior judicial experience. Professors of law, practitioners at the trial and appellate levels, political figures, as well as those with prior judicial experience have all made noteworthy careers on the bench, while others with similar professional background have not necessarily been outstanding.[13]

In the problem of ascertaining the "specific characteristics which distinguish judges with a high level of performance from those with a lower level of performance, at least three approaches are open. . . ."[14] These are the techniques of job analysis, the application of testing techniques, and the use of biographical data. Professor Rodney L. Mott, the Director of the Division of Social Sciences at Colgate University, who has long had an interest in these problems, points out the difficulties in determining through these measures the desirable specific characteristics for judicial office. As he indicates:

> "No reliable yardsticks have been developed for some of the most important attributes of judges. In spite of the optimism of some persons in high places, there is no simple, automatic, foolproof,

of one-man decisions on appeal and certain appellate court practices leading thereto. VANDERBILT, MINIMUM STANDARDS OF JUDICIAL ADMINISTRATION 438-443 (1949).
As to the need of personalities of divergent views to adjust themselves to others on the bench, consider the situation of Justice Brandeis and Chief Justice Taft on the latter's appointment to head the Supreme Court, Taft having earlier opposed the Brandeis appointment, because of the latter's "radical" views. 2 PRINGLE, THE LIFE AND TIMES OF WILLIAM HOWARD TAFT, 970-971 (1939).

[13] EWING, op. cit. supra n. 8 at 84-108, 116-119. As to prior judicial experience of state court judges see Tunstall, *Why Ignore the Bar*, 38 VA. L. REV. 1091, 1108 (1952). For criticism of the Anglo-American system "that takes a man untrained in judicial duties, puts him on the most difficult bench in the state (the trial court)" and the assumption "that trial court judicial robes will fit any competent lawyer or politician" see Marx, *Justice is Expensive*, 36 J. AM. JUD. SOC'Y 75, 76 (1952). Cf. also statement of LUMMUS, op. cit. supra n. 9, at 38: "Being a judge ought to be a career in itself, and not merely an interlude in the practice of law or the holding of political office. . . ."

[14] Mott, supra n. 5, at 264.

clean cut measure of such a basic trait as patriotism. Nor are there tests of honesty in which we have general confidence. And who would be so bold as to suggest that he has discovered a measuring rod for judicial integrity? If these important characteristics still defy measurement in the laboratory or clinic, clearly no amount of biographical data will enable us to reduce them to statistical terms."[15]

As Professor Mott has said "it may be significant"[16] that state constitutions generally fail to make specific prescriptions of character qualifications for the bench.[17]

The various states make few other requirements as to the qualifications of judges of the appellate courts and the trial courts of general jurisdiction. United States citizenship is generally required, various years of minimum residence in the state are commonly demanded, and in many states residence in the district is essential for trial judges. A minimum age from 21 to 35 is generally established for judicial office.[18] Three of the New England states, Connecticut, Massachusetts and New Hampshire, like the federal government, prescribe no legal qualifications for their judges.

## 2. *Selection of Judges*

Because of the difficulty of measuring judicial attributes objectively, we are driven inevitably in our search for the best judges to seek out the best method of selection. The first question here is how can we select judges so that they will be independent and will not be under obligation to anyone or any group for their office? Various alternatives are possible: the controlling power of selection may be lodged in the people as a whole, judges being elected by popular vote; or it may be lodged with an agency or representative of the people such as the legislature; or some particular official or officials such as the governor; or some combination of these may be entrusted with the appointment of the judiciary.

### *In England*

As we have seen, all English judges have long been appointed to office by the crown.[19] All of the judges of the County Court, the High

---

[15] *Id.* at 270.
[16] *Ibid.*
[17] Good character is required of trial judges in Arkansas and Maryland. In Maine a judge must have sobriety of manner, and in North Carolina a judge must have a belief in God. 1954-1955 BOOK OF THE STATES at 437.
[18] *Ibid.* 32 states require United States citizenship for service on the appellate courts and 34 for trial courts. Additionally trial judges in Louisiana, Minnesota, Mississippi, Missouri, Nevada, West Virginia and Wisconsin and appellate judges in Idaho and Wisconsin must be qualified voters. Required years of residence within the state vary from one to ten.
[19] Schuster, *The Office of the Lord Chancellor,* 10 CAMB. L.J. 175 (1949),

Court and the Court of Appeal and the Law Lords who exercise the appellate jurisdiction of the House of Lords, must be barristers, as we have also seen, having a certain number of years at the bar. While the justices of the peace are laymen, the stipendary magistrates who sit in certain cities are also barristers. The Prime Minister selects the Lord Chancellor who is a member of his cabinet and remains in politics while also acting as a judge. After consulting the Lord Chancellor informally he also chooses the Lord Chief Justice, the Master of the Rolls, the Law Lords, the Lord Justices of Appeal and the President of the Probate, Divorce and Admiralty Division. The Lord Chancellor, who is the head of the English judicial system, advises the Prime Minister and himself names the judges of the High Court, the County Court, the justices of the peace, and the recorders in boroughs having Courts of Quarter Sessions. Although political influences were formerly very important in such appointments, barristers who were not only of the party in power but who were active in the party having preference, the appointees were usually men of:

> "considerable professional distinction. It may indeed be suggested that this state of affairs is perhaps almost inevitable, at least with respect to the higher courts. There are sure to be acceptable men in each of the major political parties. And everyone knows who they are. Only barristers are eligible for appointment; and not only is this class itself small, but its leaders are bound to be known. They spend a large part of their time in court, in one city for the most part, and cannot help but be familiar not only to the legal profession but to many outside it. In these circumstances, one may suppose that the appointment of a man who was clearly undesirable would require a degree of effrontery of which the Ministry is not often likely to be capable. . . . Speaking now generally, it seems pretty clear that notwithstanding the intrusion of politics, the English Bench, taken as a whole, is far and away the finest body of judges in the world."[20]

In recent years the judicial caliber of the judges has become even higher.[21] In former times a judgeship came to a barrister after he had

---

points out that the Crown makes its appointments on the advice of its ministers and that the Lord Chancellor is consulted by the Prime Minister in making those appointments for which he is responsible. The Chancellor is a successful advocate usually with much experience in politics and at the bar, and well informed as to potential candidates. See remarks of Prof. Sunderland, *Cleveland Conference, Selection and Tenure of Judges in Ohio*, 8 U. CIN. L. REV. 359, 362, 364 (1934).

[20] HAYNES, SELECTION AND TENURE OF JUDGES 149-150, 154 (1944). See *id.* 136-156 for details of English practice. Ensor, Courts and Judges in France, Germany and England 82 (1933) observed: "The danger of this system is not subservience but animus. That, at different periods, a good deal of party or class prepossession has been displayed on the English bench, can scarcely be disputed."

[21] ". . . however good our laws and our legal procedure might be, the standard of the Bench is perhaps more responsible for the public reputation of our system of justice than any other factor. It is necessary to say that few who have not seen it happen would have believed the degree in which the standard of both the High

accumulated a competence if not a fortune, but with taxation what it
now is, fortunes are almost impossible to accumulate. Now as the result
of this high taxation and because of judicial pensions, men are being attracted to the bench who would never have been interested otherwise.
Next, the Lord Chancellor's advisers have been surprisingly adept in
recommending to him the right men for these high positions. In addition
respect for the courts and awareness of the threats to these institutions
in inferior partisan appointments has led to the development of a practice
in which such considerations are disregarded. Thus only two of Lord
Chancellor Jowitt's eighty-one appointees were members of the Labor
Party.[22] It has been so likewise even in some instances with the appointment of the Lord Chancellor. Thus in 1929 Prime Minister Ramsay
MacDonald selected Lord Sankey (already a judge and not of his
party) as Lord Chancellor, and Lord Sankey remained in this office
when the government became a coalition. Lord Maughan and Lord
Simonds, appointed in 1938 and 1951, had been law lords who never
had been very active in politics, although as Professor R. H. Jackson
notes "Of course a Lord Chancellor who is primarily a lawyer and
secondarily a politician must at least be in sympathy with the political
views of the cabinet in which he serves."[23] All of this has a good
effect. In this age of the common man new judges are appointed because
someone who knows his business thinks they will make good judges
and if the judges lack the colorful personality often had by the old
judges, they are likely to make up for this by being more conscientious.
The result of all this is that the English judges of today have a degree
of popular support never known by any other body of judges anywhere.
As Lord Chancellor Jowitt has put it:

" 'politics' and 'influence' (in the appointment of judges) are now completely disregarded."[24]

He ascribed this as due to the Inns of Court and the Chancellor's desire
not to provoke criticism in his Inn by the appointment of unworthy
judges, and to the practice of the Chancellor in consulting with the head
of the division of the court to which he is called upon to appoint a judge
and obtaining his approval of the appointee. The Chancellor may seek
knowledge of possible appointees where he has no personal knowledge,

---

Court and County Court Bench has steadily risen in the last quarter of a century. . . ." Gardner, *The Machinery of Law Reform in England,* 69 L.Q. REV. 46, 49 (1953).

[22] Erskine, *The Selection of Judges in England: A Standard for Comparison,* 39 A.B.A.J. 279 (1953). See HAYNES, *op. cit. supra* n. 20, at 146-150 for prior development of practices as to appointments.

[23] MACHINERY OF JUSTICE IN ENGLAND 222 (2d ed. 1953).

[24] As quoted, Erskine, *supra* n. 22 at 280. Cf. as to Canadian failure to develop a system of merit appointment and importance of political considerations, see Clark, *Appointment to the Bench,* 30 CHI. B. REV. 28 (1952).

but no letters are written by influential persons in support of a prospective nominee, no pressure is exerted on the Chancellor, and any effort to influence him is strongly disapproved. The tradition that those best qualified should be appointed and that political influence should not be important is of very recent date. In the nineteenth century politics was clearly important and it was only during the tenure in office of Lord Oxford and Asquith as prime minister from 1907 to 1916 that political considerations were first put aside.

## *In America*

In America the only matter connected with the courts which was the subject of much debate at the federal constitutional convention in 1789 was the question of the manner in which the federal judges were to be selected. The implicit recognition of the doctrine of separation of powers made the problem a delicate one. The judiciary were to be independent of the executive and the legislature in order to effectuate the system of checks and balances. Randolph's Resolution had provided for appointment by the legislature, the practice embodied in a number of contemporary state constitutions. Others spoke in favor of appointment by the executive because of various foreseeable difficulties in achieving an intelligent choice by so numerous a body as the legislature or even by one of its branches such as the Senate.[25] Finally, another one of the compromises which made the constitution possible was effected and the Constitution as adopted provided that the President "nominate and by and with the advice and consent of the Senate ... appoint ... Judges of the Supreme Court, ...."[26] Chancellor Kent said approvingly of the method finally selected:

> "The mode is peculiarly fit and proper in respect to the judiciary department.... The fittest men would probably have too much reservedness of manner, and severity of morals, to secure an election resting on universal suffrage. Nor can the mode of appointment by a large deliberative assembly be entitled to unqualified approbation. There are too many occasions, and too much temptation for intrigue, party prejudice, and local interest, to permit such a body of men to act, in respect to such appointment, with a sufficiently single and steady regard for the general welfare...."[27]

In the sixteen decades since the Constitution was adopted, as politics have threatened to engulf the federal courts and particularly the Supreme

---

[25] For details see HARRIS, THE ADVICE AND CONSENT OF THE SENATE 17-25 (1953); WARREN, THE MAKING OF THE CONSTITUTION 326-329, 531-532, 641 (1928).
[26] U.S. CONSTITUTION, Art. II, sec. 2, cl. 2. For discussion see THE FEDERALIST, Nos. 76, 77 (Hamilton).
[27] I Commentaries on American Law 291, Part II, Lecture XIV (14th ed. Gould 1896).

Court, changes in the method of appointment have been suggested at times, but no alterations have ever been effectuated in the mode of selecting the federal judiciary.[28]

The years from 1830 to the Civil War were a period of rapid and vast change in the life of the country, accompanied by radical political and constitutional developments, often denominated the Jacksonian Revolution. The elimination of property qualifications and extension of the suffrage to all men was accompanied by a belief in rotation in office and the development of the spoils system.[29] As popular election was extended to the presidency, so it was extended to other officials who had once been appointed by the legislature or the governor:[30] "the wave of democratic fervor that was sweeping over the world tended in America to bring nearly all public officers under direct popular control, the judges among the rest."[31] Many states adopted provisions for filling judicial office by popular election; the "mode of selection by legislature or by the governor and the legislature was widely condemned as introducing the evils of party politics into judicial appointments. It was openly asserted that judicial places were becoming the spoils of partisan conflict and selections were made not on account of ability and fitness but as rewards for political services. To overcome this evil the selection of judges directly by the electorate was declared to be the only remedy."[32]

---

[28] CARPENTER, JUDICIAL TENURE IN THE UNITED STATES 185-186 (1918). As recently as the first decade of this century Walter Clark, Chief Justice of the North Carolina Supreme Court, conducted a campaign to have federal judges elected. See Sen. Doc. No. 610, 63d Cong. 2d Sess. (1914). In the presidential campaign of 1924 one of the planks of LaFollette's platform was to make the federal judiciary elective. BEMAN, ELECTION V. APPOINTMENT OF JUDGES 24, 116-117 (1926).

[29] HAYNES, *op. cit. supra* n. 20, at 88-89, as to the spoils system see SCHLESINGER, THE AGE OF JACKSON 45-47 (1946).

[30] In four of the thirteen original states judges were appointed by the governor subject to the consent of the council. In New York judges were named by a Special Council of Appointment consisting of the governor and certain members of the legislature. In the remaining original states judges were selected by one or both houses of the legislature. See HAYNES, *op. cit. supra* n. 20, at 105-108, 115, 121-128, 133 (1944).

[31] *Id.* at 90. Vermont was the first state to provide for popular election of some judges above the rank of justices of the peace, and in 1812 judges of certain inferior courts in Georgia were so elected. By 1845 only Indiana and Michigan also had made provisions for popular election of some of their judges, and only in Mississippi were all judges so elected. In 1846 New York provided for popular election of all judges and within ten years 15 of the 29 states existing in 1846 had followed suit. All of the states that entered the union after 1846 have provided for popularly elected judges. *Id.* 99-100; Aumann, *op. cit. supra* n. 2 at 185-189.

[32] Carpenter, *op. cit. supra* n. 28, at 171-172. The movement for popular election was closely related to the abolition of tenure during good behavior and substitution for it of a term for a period of years—*Id.* at 178. See POUND, CRIMINAL JUSTICE IN AMERICA 134-135 (1945) ascribing these changes to disputes over judicial review of constitutional questions. Other causes have been assigned for these radical changes; *e.g.*: dissatisfaction with decisions against the debtor classes (Carpenter, *op. cit. supra* at 172); the development of party politics and a desire

At present in the federal courts, and in Delaware, Maine, Massachusetts, New Hampshire and New Jersey, the majority of all judges are appointed by the executive subject to confirmation by some body such as the senate or governor's council, while in Rhode Island trial court judges are so appointed. In several other states various classes of judges are appointed.[33] All judges with some minor exceptions are selected by popular vote in thirty-six states, in twenty of which they are elected under party labels.[34]

In many of the states where judicial offices are nominally filled by the legislature or by popular election many judges originally receive their commissions to office by virtue of *ad interim* appointments by the governor. These *ad interim* appointees as a class are better than the judges nominated in partisan contests. When they run for election at the end of their appointments, the prestige of their position frequently insures their election. In this manner the caliber of the elected judiciary is vastly improved. It is rather generally conceded that the elective system would long since have proved unworkable in practice had it not been that in state after state a majority of judges owe their original selection to such *ad interim* appointments.[35]

---

to increase the available "spoils" (Perry, *Politics and Judicial Administration*, 109 ANNALS 75, 78 (1933); a guess may be hazarded that the low level of ability of early judges and their failure to conduct themselves judiciously helped the movement for popular election. For contemporary views see REPORT OF DEBATES AND PROCEEDINGS OF THE CONVENTION FOR THE REVISION OF THE CONSTITUTION OF NEW YORK (Bishop & Attree 1846) 141-142, 410, 582-585; REPORT OF DEBATES AND PROCEEDINGS OF THE CONVENTION FOR REVISION OF THE CONSTITUTION OF OHIO, 1850-51, Vol. I at 86, Vol. II at 355.

[33] VANDERBILT, *op. cit. supra* n. 12 at 6. For instances of appointment by the governor in Florida, Georgia, South Carolina, and Vermont, see *ibid*.

[34] 1954-1955 BOOK OF THE STATES 436. In addition most trial court judges are elected in California and Missouri (the appellate judges of which states are selected under a special plan, see *infra* at pp. 46, 47). See also for special instances of elected judges VANDERBILT, *op. cit. supra* n. 12 at 10.

[35] *Id.* at 8. See also tables of information regarding judges in the highest state courts in Tunstall, *Why Ignore the Bar*, 38 VA. L. REV. 1091, 1099, 1108 (1952). In the 36 states in which there is popular election Tunstall indicates 106 of the 233 judges of the highest state courts then in office were originally appointed to office. In the 5 states in which judges are elected by the legislature 10 of the 27 were originally appointed. And the appendix to this article indicates that as of 1952 in states where judges nominally are elected by the people or the legislature, a majority of the judges of the highest court had originally been appointed in Ala., Colo., Fla., Ga., Idaho, Mich., Minn., Nev., N. Car., Ore., S. Dak., Tex., Vt., Va., Wash., Wis., and Wyo. *Id.* at 1108-1109. In Wisconsin 30 of the 47 justices who have served on the Supreme Court were originally selected by appointment. The duration of the appointments varied from one month to six years. 1953 BIENNIAL REPORT OF WISCONSIN JUDICIAL COUNCIL 62, 65. 42% of the Wisconsin circuit judges were originally selected by appointment. *Id.* at 70. In Minnesota the constant reelection of incumbents has meant that offices are usually vacated by death or retirement for age or health, giving the governor frequent opportunity for ad interim appointments. The result has been that a large majority of the judges are originally appointed by the governor. In 1941 three quarters of the district court judges obtained office originally by such appointment. Moos, *Judicial Election and Partisan Endorsement of Judicial Candidates in Minnesota*, 35 AM. POL. SCI. REV. 69, 70 (1941).

In contrast to the present state of affairs in England partisan politics continue to play a large role in the selection of judges in the United States. In this country almost from the beginning appointments to offices traditionally have been the reward for party service. Where appointments are not used as a direct prize for such activity they are an indirect recognition of the appointee's political views as evidenced by his membership in the party, or of the services of some other party member who favors the appointee.[36]

In adjudging the method of selection of judges for the federal courts it is proper to distinguish between appointments to the Supreme Court[37] and those to the lower federal courts. Because of the importance of the Supreme Court in the constitutional scheme and the dramatic consequences of its decisions in certain fields the limelight of popular interest is focused on appointments to that court. While it is an aforegone conclusion that appointees will generally be of the dominant political party,[38] the merit of the appointees is subjected to much thought and examination and the President will rarely propose and the Senate rarely approve an obviously unfit candidate.[39] In the appointment of judges to the district courts and the courts of appeal it cannot be expected that public attention will be so great. Local political influence is predominant. Although the President is supposedly free in his choice, senatorial wishes are in reality controlling in most appointments particularly in the district courts.[40] And yet it has justly been said that the

---

[36] Evans, *Political Influences in the Selection of Federal Judges*, 1948 WIS. L. REV. 330, one of the most thorough examinations of the political affiliations of federal judicial appointees since the time of Grover Cleveland, indicating an almost 100% identification between the party membership of those appointed and the appointing President. See also Shartel, *Federal Judges, Appointment, Supervision and Removal*, 28 MICH. L. REV. 485 (1930). As to the importance of political considerations in Canada see Clark, *supra* n. 24.

[37] For a detailed discussion of Supreme Court appointments see Ewing, *op. cit. supra* n. 8 at 12-40. See also HARRIS, THE ADVICE AND CONSENT OF THE SENATE 99-114, 302-305 (1953).

[38] President Truman's appointment of Republican Senator Burton to the Supreme Court is a recent exception which proves the rule. See also WRIGHT, GROWTH OF AMERICAN CONSTITUTIONAL LAW 248 (1942); Frank, *The Appointment of Supreme Court Justices; Prestige, Principles and Politics*, 1941 WIS. L. REV. 172, 343, 461.

[39] Ewing, *op. cit. supra* n. 8, examination of biographical data reveals the importance of political and official antecedents of Supreme Court appointments at 101-102, 116-,117. Similarly, Frank, *supra* n. 38. The duty of investigating candidates for judicial office is entrusted to the Department of Justice, CUMMINGS AND MCFARLAND, FEDERAL JUSTICE 529 (1937).

[40] See Harris, *op. cit. supra* n. 37 at 314-324; Evans, *supra* n. 36; Sears, *The Appointment of Federal District Judges*, 25 ILL. L. REV. 54 (1930) for details of an appointment of a district judge in Pennsylvania by President Hoover indicating that the president and attorney general were guided by the Pennsylvania senator's recommendation; Sears, *A Minnesota Judgeship*, 26 ILL. L. REV. 121 (1931), reporting an instance in which the Attorney General did not approve of the Minnesota senator's recommendation and a bar association poll was also recorded against the senator's nominee. The author of these articles was quite

"federal judiciary is the best evidence we have of the virtues and faults of the method of judicial selection of which the federal system is typical. . . . It seems to be universally agreed that the federal judges, as a group, are a better body of judges than those of any state. . . ."[41]

Political influences on appointments are of prime importance not only in the federal courts but in all the states where judges are appointed.[42] In most states in which judges are not elected partisan considerations play an important role in the selection of the judiciary and in appointments to the lower courts local political interests are favored.[43] One of the ways of decreasing the political pressures on the appointing power is to provide for bipartisan appointments under which appointments must be divided between the major parties. In Delaware the constitution requires that not more than a bare majority of all its judges be from one political party.[44] In New Hampshire vacancies are filled so as to

---

critical of the practice by which ". . . appointments to the federal district bench are matters of patronage with reference to which the President infringes upon the customary prerogatives of the Senators from any particular state whenever he refuses to appoint the persons selected by two particular Senators. . . ." *Id.* at 136. In this particular instance the Senator finally abandoned his nomination and sent the President a list of individuals who would be satisfactory to him, but President Hoover responded by saying it was too late to investigate these individuals and instead submitted a list to the senator and simultaneously sent in a nomination to the Senate.

Erskine, *supra* n. 22 at 348, puts it this way: "In practice the senators of a state who are members of the party in power in effect appoint the federal district judges sitting in their state and subject to a power of veto of the President, and where neither senator of a state belongs to the President's party, the leaders of that party in the state in effect make the appointment subject to the same veto."

A recent battle between the President and a senator involved former President Harry S. Truman and Senator Paul Douglas of Illinois. Senator Douglas, whose recommendation met with the approval of the Chicago Bar Association, denounced the President's appointees as "contrary to the public interest and in that sense personally obnoxious to me." TIME, August 6, 1951, p. 6; HARRIS, *op. cit. supra* n. 37, at 215-216. See as to very recent appointment problems, TIME, October 12, 1953, at p. 18. As to examples of senatorial influence see speech by Senator Smith of New Jersey, 97 CONG. REC. 3476, 3477-78 (1951).

[41] HAYNES, *op. cit. supra* n. 20 at 19. This statement is supported by the findings of Mott, Albright and Semmerling, *supra* n. 8, at 149-154.

[42] VANDERBILT, *op. cit. supra* n. 12, at 9; cf. the very interesting provision of the first Maryland Constitution of 1776, Art. L, which provided: "That the Governor, every member of the Council, and every Judge and Justice, before they act as such, shall respectively take an oath, 'That he will not, through favor, affection or partiality vote for any person to office; and that he will vote for such person as, in his judgment and conscience, he believes most fit and qualified for the office'. . . ." The first Tennessee Constitution of 1796, Art. IX, sec. 2 exacted a similar oath of its legislators who were entrusted with the selection of judges. With these it is interesting to compare the reply of Senator Lodge to President T. Roosevelt's letter assessing the views of a prospective justice: "I do not see why Republicans cannot be found who hold these opinions as well as Democrats. The fact that there have been one or two Republican disappointments does not seem to me to militate against the proposition." as quoted in CUMMINGS & MCFARLAND, *op. cit. supra* n. 39, at 528.

[43] *E.g.* MOLEY, TRIBUNES OF THE PEOPLE, THE PAST AND PRESENT OF THE NEW YORK MAGISTRATE'S COURTS 35, 219-220 (1932); WARNER & CABOT, JUDGES AND LAW REFORM 11, 182-185 (1936).

[44] DEL. CONST., Art. 4, sec. 3, as amended 47 Del. Laws, c. 177 (1949), 48 Del. Laws, c. 109 (1951).

maintain both the political and geographical balance of the courts.[45] In New Jersey an unwritten tradition dictating bipartisan selection of judicial officers started nearly a hundred years ago in the supreme court has continued and has been gradually extended to all courts.[46] Bipartisan appointments are an excellent way of proving to the public that one party does not control the courts and that the courts are not in politics.

In practice many differences have developed in the operation of the elective system of selecting judges in the thirty-six states where most judges are so chosen. Many devices have been experimented with in the century since the elective principle was first applied to in attempts to safeguard the democratic process and to eliminate partisan pressures.[47] On the whole such measures have been unsuccessful. In some states particularly in the lower courts judicial office is merely a rung on the political ladder and the turnover in judicial office is tremendous. In many states in order to obtain judicial office a candidate must not only participate in a party campaign, but must almost constantly be active in party politics,[48] and is subject to being defeated along with his party, or for an unpopular decision, or for reasons not fundamentally connected with his judicial performance.[49] Unfortunately despite much good will and earnest effort partisan pressures predominate wherever judges are elected, "the selection of a judge by this method is not only influenced by politics; it is politics itself."[50]

---

[45] VANDERBILT, *op. cit. supra* n. 12, at 9. Vacancies there have customarily been filled by appointment of a lawyer of the same party as was he who vacated the office and the bench is not overwhelmingly packed with members of the party of the appointing power. This practice dates back only to the last decades of the nineteenth century. For detailed history of the nineteenth century and account of frequent politically inspired changes in the courts and judicial personnel, see CORNING, *The Highest Courts of Law in New Hampshire,* 2 G.B. 469 (1890).

[46] This is a matter of practice as to the Supreme and Superior Courts but is required by statute in the appointment of county judges where there are several judges in the county. N.J. REV. STAT., Tit. 2A:3-14 (1952). See speech by Senator Smith of New Jersey, 97 Cong. Rec. 3473, 3475 (1951).

[47] For survey of practices involved in the nomination and election of judges see VANDERBILT, *op. cit. supra* n. 12 at 10-11; Feightner, *Judicial Selection and Tenure,* 15 IND. L.J. 215 (1940). As to lack of effectiveness of nonpartisan ballots in Ohio see n. 70 *infra.* As to those states in which incumbent judges are habitually returned to office see VANDERBILT, *op. cit. supra* n. 12 at 20-21.

[48] Cf. as to political activities of elected judges VANDERBILT, *op. cit. supra* n. 12, at 15-16; McCoy, *Judicial Selection and Judicial Conduct,* 24 So. CALIF. L. REV. 1, 17-23 (1950). For the experience in particular states see MARTIN, *op. cit. supra* n. 8, at 272-288; Aumann, *Selection, Tenure and Retirement of Judges in Ohio,* 5 U. CIN. L. REV. 408 (1931); Fox, *Judges and Politics,* 27 TEMP. L.Q. 1 (1953).

[49] See BALDWIN, THE AMERICAN JUDICIARY 317-320 (1905); Martin, *op. cit. supra* n. 8 at 190-193; Bryant, *Supreme Court of Wisconsin,* 9 G.B. 213, 218 (1897); Thornton, *Supreme Court of Indiana,* 4 G.B. 207, 233, 249 (1892).

[50] Erskine, *supra* n. 22 at 348. Fox, *supra* n. 48 at 2 recently observed that in Pennsylvania "Judges get and hold their commissions 'at the pleasure of political bosses.'"

One of the most enlightening examinations of the evils of the elective system in practice is Edward Martin's detailed study of Chicago's judicial elections.[51] Published in 1936 this book indicates the many problems which beset the elective method of selection everywhere, and which are presented in exaggerated degree in that sprawling industrial and commercial metropolis where the game of politics has never been a clean one. There a "total of eighty-eight judges is elected to sit on the nine separate tribunals of city or county-wide jurisdiction, which serve a population of nearly four million persons. These judges are chosen by an electorate of more than one and one-half million voters, approximately 85% of whom reside within the City of Chicago."[52] In the period from 1887 to 1934 the recommendations of the organized profession, the Bar Association, were often disregarded.[53] Only a small percentage of the Chicago electorate voted in its special judicial elections while a large number of voters fail to mark their ballots for judicial offices which are part of the regular ballot as in Presidential election years.[54] Party organizations occupy a primary position in the selection of judges as a result of the two-party tradition, the development of permanent organizations within the major parties to manage electoral

---

[51] MARTIN, THE ROLE OF THE BAR IN ELECTING THE BENCH IN CHICAGO (Ph.D. dissertation, U. of Chicago, 1936) examines in detail the successive judicial elections in that city.

[52] *Id.* at 11. One judge holds office for 9 years, two serve for 4 years, and the remaining 88 judges have 6-year terms. See Table II, *id.* at 15, for list of 165 officials for which a typical Chicagoan votes. To nominate and elect a single set of these 88 judges the voter is expected to go to the polls eight times. See Table IV *id.* at 17 for Cycles of Judicial Elections in Chicago. Thus 88 judges of the six civil courts are elected in nine different groups and in six independent cycles, in four of these groups judicial elections are held simultaneously with contests for other offices. In one particular six-year cycle there were 423 candidates for 146 judicial offices in 18 different elections to be considered by each voter. *Id.* 18. See as to situation in Detroit area and Wayne County, VIRTUE, *op. cit. supra* n. 4, at 63-67. In Detroit the entire bench of three courts, thirty judges, come up for election in one year although at separate elections. The nonpartisan ballot has resulted in what is known as "name" candidacies, the running of unknown persons with names identical or confusingly similar to those with established records.

[53] Only 70% of the judges elected were endorsed by the Bar Association, 80% of the incumbent judges sought reelection and 80% of these were endorsed by the Bar Association but only 63% were reelected. The Bar Association's disapproval of certain judges running for reelection seemed to have little effect resulting in only 41 defeats in a list of 67 such candidacies by 16 different incumbents. MARTIN, *op. cit. supra* n. 51 at 192-193. Chart IV at 189 analyzes comparatively party successes and defeats. The influence of national political tides on the success of candidates for the Municipal Court at the polls is discussed. *Id.* 190-191.

[54] *Id.* at 211-214. The inertia among the electorate is ascribed by Martin to Chicago's long ballot. See Chart VI at 215 for graphic portrayal of voters' oversight of judicial offices for regular elections. For recent criticism of the long ballot see Klots, *The Selection of Judges and the Short Ballot*, 10 THE RECORD 103 (1955). Note also the cogent observation in THE FEDERALIST, No. 76 (Hamilton): "The exercise of it (the power of appointment) by the people at large will be readily admitted to be impracticable; as waiving every other consideration, it would leave them little time to do anything else."

matters, the entrenched positions of the parties as a matter of law, and the system of sponsoring candidates used by powerful politicians. The use of a coalition ticket, a frequent practice, was cited as making the individual's ballot "an empty and futile gesture,"[55] since the voter was thus deprived of even a chance between two party sponsored candidates. The prior careers of the successful candidates indicated that before running for judicial posts the overwhelming majority had been in offices that were controlled by political parties. "No one knows any better than the judges themselves, however, that it is the politicians who elect them today . . . in Chicago the party machines, not judicial records, control elections."[56]

The difficulty of the public as a whole in getting to know and judge the qualifications of many practitioners of law in the rush of life in today's predominantly urban society presents a major obstacle to the effective use of the elective process. Moreover, judges are not essentially representatives of the people as are legislators and the executive.[57] The experience of the past years and the many abuses of the elective process which have developed indicates that the nomination of judges thereunder will be the work of a few irresponsible party leaders. How is the judicial candidate to campaign effectively for office? What is the platform on which he may stand? What may he validly promise?[58] Political cam-

---

[55] MARTIN, *op. cit. supra* n. 51 at 250. While a coalition ticket included some able incumbents, it also made possible the election of some the "Bar primary had stamped as utterly unfit." *Id.* at 99.

[56] *Id.* 251-252, 257-258. Martin concluded that the efforts of the Bar Association to improve judicial selection had had few tangible results. *Id.* 175-211, 235-247, 362-364.

[57] See Wilkins, *The Judicial Function and the Error of Electing Judges*, 8 OKLA. STATE B.J. 185 (1933); "The purpose of a court is not to give effect to the popular will but to declare the law. . . ." To similar effect see BOK, n. 58, *infra*.

[58] In BOK'S BACKBONE OF THE HERRING (1941), the judge who originally received an ad interim appointment in his first campaign for election could do little since open electioneering was not done, "but there were things to be done beneath the surface. He (the candidate) did these with ardor, trying to make friends and establish contacts in doubtful precincts, telephoning endlessly and conferring in chambers. . . . His judicial work lagged somewhat during this period. He was not expected to handle cases of public interest: it was too easy to make enemies and to expose himself to improper pressure. He was able to avoid situations of that kind, even though he once had to resort to a slight taxi accident in order to make him late enough for court and ensure the threatening case being reassigned for trial. . . . The end, with the campaign in full swing, appeared not only to justify the means but to require them." At 44-45. Cf. the same judge's feelings when his term again expired and he came up before the voters. He refused to make the usual necessary gesture to the opposition party which as a sitting judge would have entitled him to their endorsement, explaining that "Part of our duty as judges is the use of power over others. We are lost if we think it is our power that we use. It is given to us by them to preserve their peace and to teach them when they no longer see how to keep their own. They give it to us to settle wars between them. How can we do it if there is war within us? Our power is the gentleness and understanding and awareness with which we use their gift. We cannot fight for it. We cannot even ask for it, for asking means that

paigns are costly and if a judge must participate in such a campaign, how is he to escape sharing the costs, directly or indirectly?[59]

The basic criticism directed at the elective system is that, linked as it is with tenure for a term of years necessitating repeated stands before the electorate, it lessens the independence of the judiciary by making politics a primary element in their selection and continuance in office.[60] Unqualified and inferior men are often elected judges in a system which is permeated by politics especially in cosmopolitan communities. Where political connections are necessary to become a judge, many lawyers do not wish to become candidates because they do not wish to be involved in what is so often, in this respect, a very "dirty game". Where the populace cannot in most cases make a valid judgment on the merits of the many judicial nominees on the ballot,[61] the judges are not really elected but are appointed by political leaders[62] whom the public often

---

we are hungry, and a hungry man first asks and then demands. Who can demand anything and remain gentle? No. This gift of power comes as a duty laid before our feet. If we seek it, we give away ourselves and then we are lost indeed, lost and dangerous, like a child with dynamite and fire." *Id.* at 291. See also In re Strahl, 201 App. Div. 729, 195 N.Y. Supp. 385 (2d Dept. 1922).

[59] BRUCE, THE AMERICAN JUDGE 142-143 (1924). If a judge is not sufficiently wealthy to bear such costs, he must raise the money somehow and in doing so he must become obligated. See as to campaign assessments MARTIN, *op. cit. supra* n. 51, at 256-258.

[60] See Kales, *Methods of Selecting and Retiring Judges,* 11 J. AM. JUD. SOC'Y 133, 134 (1928). "It is one of our most absurd bits of political hypocrisy that we actually talk and act as if our judges were elected when the method of selection is, in form, by popular election . . . (in Chicago judges) are appointed. The appointing power is lodged with the leaders of the party machines. These men appoint the nominees. They did it openly and with a certain degree of responsibility under the convention system. They do it now less openly and with less responsibility under our compulsory and partisan primary system."

"In the cold morning after we wonder how many voters remember the names of the judges they voted for on Tuesday. Well, not many. Once again an examination of results—generally good in themselves but based almost wholly on blind adherence to political party label—shows that the selection process is all wrong. The public simply does not have the qualifications to determine the qualifications of men for the bench.

"What criterion did the public use in voting for the thirty-three places on the bench filled by New York City voters? Political party seems, so far as we can see, the only standard for judgment. Take the Court of Appeals, for instance. Where there was a chance to go astray (that is, where a candidate was not endorsed by both major parties) the voters ignored bar association grading of candidates. The real contest lay between Presiding Justice Sydney F. Foster of the Appellate Division, Third Department, and Adrian P. Burke, Corporation Counsel of New York City. The Bar Association of the City of New York and the New York County Lawyers Association called Judge Foster 'outstandingly qualified,' The Bronx Bar Association 'well qualified.' All three graded Mr. Burke as 'qualified.' Mr. Burke, a Democrat with Liberal endorsement, won. The conclusion is inescapable that he was carried in by the Harriman-Democratic votes. We say this without criticism of Mr. Burke. Everywhere else, among the judgeships, the voting was by political party. N.Y. *Times,* November 4, 1954, p. 30.

[61] See Rufus Choate's famous observations on this in 1853: *Judicial Tenure,* 17 J. AM. JUD. SOC'Y 10 (1933). See also LOWELL, PUBLIC OPINION AND POPULAR GOVERNMENT 105-109, 260-261 (1926).

[62] Kales made this observation in 1914, *supra* n. 60. For concurrence by a popu-

does not know and over whom it has no real control. Criticism has been levelled at the direct primary, the voters' lack of knowledge of the qualifications of the candidates,[63] the failure to vote where special elections or a nonpartisan separate ballot were provided,[64] and the elimination of the voter's choice by the use of the bipartisan coalition endorsement.[65] The resultant deterioration in the quality of the bench, moreover, has led to an increasing reliance on administrative agencies.[66] The major defect of the elective system is that it renders judges subservient[67] in the same way that English judges were before the Act of Settlement, since in a sense they hold office only during pleasure, for a term, and are subject to dismissal for political or other invalid reasons. As Chief Justice Stone, then Dean at Columbia University School of Law, stated in 1915:

> "There can be little doubt that the substitution of the elective for the appointive system has, on the whole, had an evil effect upon both the American bench and bar. Too often its practical operation has been to substitute for the choice of the responsible executive the choice of the irresponsible political boss or wire-puller. . . . The whole tendency is to substitute political availability for proved probity and skill as a test of qualification for judicial office. . . ."[68]

---

lar politician see ALFRED SMITH, THE CITIZEN AND HIS GOVERNMENT 85-86 (1935). See also Love, *Judicial Selection and Tenure*, 1952 U. ILL. L. FORUM 542, 545.

"It may, however, be asked, why should a popular election produce a worse Bench than appointment by an Executive, seeing that the Executive is . . . chosen by a political party and disposed to serve its interests. Why then should a Prime Minister be any more likely to make good appointments than a party organization? If the boss of an American State party organization is a party man, so is a State Governor, so is the President of the United States himself. The explanation is that the President is responsible to the Nation, and the Governor to his State. Either official would damage himself and his party if he made bad appointments, whereas the party machine has no official character, and cannot be made responsible for what is legally the act of the voters when they elect a person whom the Machine has put forward as a candidate." BRYCE, II MODERN DEMOCRACIES 387-388 (1921).

[63] As to the reality of the lack of knowledge of voters about their judicial candidates when found as a ballot in which 26 vacancies were to be filled, twenty of which were for judicial office, Klots, *The Selection of Judges and the Short Ballot*, 10 THE RECORD 103 (1955) has some startling facts.

[64] Brand, *Selection of Judges—The Fiction of Majority Elections*, 34 J. AM. JUD. SOC'Y 136, 140 (1951).

[65] See n. 55 *supra*. See also, *New York Experience Shows Need for Better Methods of Choosing Judges*, 29 A.B.A.J. 690 (1943).

[66] McCormick, *Judicial Selection—Current Plans and Trends*, 30 ILL. L. REV. 446 (1935).

[67] Note De Tocqueville's prescience in this matter, I DEMOCRACY IN AMERICA 279 (Reeve ed. Bowen rev., 1945).

[68] LAW AND ITS ADMINISTRATION 184-185 (1915). Dean Stone went on the say: "It is indeed remarkable that with a system so fraught with possibilities of public injury we have escaped to so great a degree actual corruption and public scandal. It is true that judges in New York, as an aftermath of the Tweed Ring exposures, were impeached and removed from office for corrupt practices; but the charges to be laid at the door of our elective system is rather that it has resulted in a lowering in tone and professional character of both bench and bar, and has deprived the bench of that leadership and public confidence to which it should be legitimately entitled. . . ." at 186.

Political influences in the making and unmaking of elected judges are self-evident. The elimination of such partisan considerations and the establishment of a system of selection based on merit is the basic aim of all who are interested in improving the administration of justice. It is possible, of course, for undesirable political influences to be eliminated from both an appointive and an elective system. Primarily the vigilance of public opinion must be mobilized by an enlightened bar. Measures to eliminate politics such as the non-partisan ballot[69] are in themselves insufficient without effective public support and participation.[70] Public education in these matters is fundamental for the achievement and functioning of any reform, otherwise what is started as a reform may be so subjected to abuse as to become a tool to increase political influence. In this process the bar must play its part. Through its organizations,[71] the bar can advise the public as to the qualifications of those who are being considered. More important, the bar must help to educate the public to an awareness of their responsibilities and the dangers inherent in partisan influences in the selection of the judiciary both under the elective and the appointive systems.

The problems to be resolved in achieving the best possible mode of selection of judges are many. The elective and appointive system each have their proponents pointing out particular instances where the system has worked well in practice. As one keen observer has put it:

> "Whether judges should be elected or appointed is a political question and in all honesty ought to be treated as such. You may take the controlling power of selection from one group or individual and vest it in another but you cannot abolish it. There simply is no such

---

[69] In Minnesota from 1912 to 1941 all judges have been nominated and elected without partisan designation. This has been said to have resulted in a well qualified bench. Incumbent judges are usually continued in office. Only one supreme court judge since 1912 was defeated at the polls and of the 84 district judges who served in this period, only 4 were defeated in campaigns for reelection. Since many judges owed their office to ad interim appointments, it was observed that "In Minnesota, the nomination and election of judges on nonpartisan ballots has actually been a plan of filling judicial posts by executive appointment, with popular ratification." For details of Minnesota experience see Moos, *supra* n. 35.

[70] *E.g.*, see agreement of Newton D. Baker and Senator Burton of Ohio that they did the people of Ohio a disservice when they drew the nonpartisan primary law of Ohio. *Cincinnati Conference, Selection and Tenure of Judges in Ohio*, 8 U. CIN. L. REV. 359, 482 (1934).

[71] See generally as to possible activities of the bar association and ways in which to make its leadership most effectual, RUTHERFORD, THE INFLUENCE OF THE AMERICAN BAR ASSOCIATION ON PUBLIC OPINION AND LEGISLATION (1937); MARTIN, *op. cit. supra* n. 51 at 175-247, 360-364. See as to effectiveness of American Bar Association's campaign against judicial recall, RUTHERFORD, 142-153; and of activities in the selection of judges, *id.* at 155-161. In 1946, a Special Committee on the Judiciary was created by the American Bar Association to study and recommend action regarding nominees to the federal courts. 30 J. AM. JUD. SOC'Y 66 (1946). Cf. as to effect of bar association action the campaign against Frieda Hennock which led to the withdrawal of her name for one of the vacancies in the federal district court. 7 THE RECORD 359 (1952).

thing as automatic selection of any public officer except where the office is hereditary. Any system which places the power of selecting judges or other officials in the hands of human beings or a group of humans is political. Every person who is or hopes to be in office is in politics."[72]

Dissatisfaction continues, however, and there is a general desire for higher standards for the judiciary who occupy such an important place in the American scheme of things. This has led to the evolution of compromise plans which seek to utilize the best features of the elective and appointive systems.[73] In 1937 the American Bar Association approved a plan of judicial selection as a substitute for direct election.[74] This plan provides for appointment by the governor, such appointment being restricted to a list proposed by a specially constituted commission or board comprised of lawyers and laymen. The appointee at the end of a certain period and all incumbents at the expiration of their terms, must then stand for election on a ballot on which the voter may answer only in the affirmative or in the negative the question of whether or not the judge should be retained in office. While appointment to judicial office rests with the executive originally, his discretion is limited, and the appointee at the end of a certain period is subjected to a popular vote. Although final control is exercised by the electorate the difficulties resulting from partisan pressures are eliminated. An early version of a similar plan has been in operation in California for the selection of appellate court judges since 1934. In California the governor with the requisite approval of a special Commission on Qualifications makes the necessary appointment,[75] and after a period of service on the bench the judge's name is submitted to the people for approval or rejection. In Missouri the plan approved by the American Bar Association has been adopted but applies only to the appellate courts and certain trial courts in the larger cities[76] and in Alabama this plan has been applied

---

[72] Fisher, *Selection of Cook County Judges*, 31 ILL. L. REV. 898 (1937). The author, Chief Justice of the Circuit Court of Cook County, believed that "The elective method at least offers the remote possibility of an aroused public making the ultimate choice."

[73] For excellent short historical and critical summaries, see Brand, *supra* n. 64; Winters, *A Better Way to Select Our Judges*, 34 J. AM. JUD. SOC'Y 166 (1951). For a recent suggestion see Bloch, *The Selection of Judges: The Independence of the Federal Courts*, 41 A.B.A.J. 507 (1955).

[74] 62 A.B.A. REP. 893-897 (1937). See A.B.A. HANDBOOK ON THE IMPROVEMENT OF THE ADMINISTRATION OF JUSTICE 80-83 (3d ed. 1952). Campaigns for adoption of this plan are being carried on in many of the states. Elliott, *Judicial Administration*, 29 N.Y.U.L.Q. REV. 155, 157-160 (1954); 1954-1955 BOOK OF THE STATES 432. For origin of this plan in Prof. Kales' suggestion of 1914 see Winters, *supra* n. 73 at 170.

[75] Calif. Const., Art. VI, sec. 26, as added 1934. As to history of this provision and appointments under this method see Smith, *The California Method of Selecting Judges*, 3 STAN. L. REV. 571 (1951).

[76] Mo. CONST., Art. 5, secs. 29(a)-(g) (1945). For examination of the application of these provisions see Pelatson, *The Missouri Plan for the Selection of*

in one court.[77] The essence of these plans is a combination of features of the appointive and elective systems in order to provide selection by qualified and responsible personnel while entrusting to the electorate a final voice in such selection. Under these plans also the influences of partisan politics is kept at a minimum, since the nominating commission is not composed of party representatives and when the judge comes before the electorate he is not on a party ticket.

## On the Continent

On the Continent, where judges form a separate profession or special branch of the civil service[78] and are specially trained for the office, the holding of judicial office is a career[79] and the problem of selection is different from that in the common-law countries. The French judiciary, the staff of the Ministry of Justice and the parquet, the state's attorney who appear in the courts, form one group who move from rung to rung on the promotional ladder in any of the three departments. Although it is common to speak of the judicial profession of France as distinguished from other legal careers, the highest judgeships may be conferred on men who have not necessarily had many years of judicial experience, but instead have spent the greater part of their time on the parquet or in the Ministry of Justice.[80] It is the manipulation of desirable judicial promotions that presents difficulties on the Continent since "The promise of promotion may easily be used to obtain a judiciary subservient to the executive authority . . . it is everywhere conceded that the prospect of promotion undermines the independence of the judiciary."[81] At least one expert concluded, however, that "the European method of examination and apprenticeship is more successful in drafting competent and honest inferior court judges than is the American method of leaving the choice of magistrates to ward politicians."[82]

## The Appropriate Method

The method of best selecting the best judges is one which must always be determined in the light of history and local conditions.[83] Tradition

---

*Judges* (20 U. OF MO. STUDIES, No. 2, 1945). See also Hyde, *Missouri Plan for Selection and Tenure of Judges,* 9 F.R.D. 457 (1949) indicating the success of this plan in freeing judicial selection from politics. An appendix, *id.* at 464-465, indicates that even when the popular vote was generally Republican judges affiliated with the Democrats were retained in office and vice versa.

[77] Circuit Court of Birmingham, 34 J. AM. JUD. SOC'Y 120 (1950).

[78] Crabites, *The French Civil Bench From Within,* 14 A.B.A.J. 572 (1928).

[79] See ENSOR, COURTS AND JUDGES IN FRANCE, GERMANY AND ENGLAND (1933); Garner, *The French Judiciary,* 26 YALE L.J. 348 (1917).

[80] Ensor, *op. cit. supra* n. 79, at 28, 115-118.

[81] Ploscowe, *The Career of Judges and Prosecutors in Continental Countries,* 44 YALE L. REV. 268, 275, 289 (1931).

[82] *Id.* at 291.

[83] See generally, BEMAN, ELECTION VERSUS APPOINTMENT OF JUDGES 9-25, 37-160 (1926); Bibliography on these problems, HAYNES, SELECTION AND TENURE OF

and current practices may do much to alleviate actual defects in a system. In New Jersey, where the governor is a political official with the usual party obligations, a tradition of bipartisanship has resulted in the elimination of the purely political appointment in many instances where the governor is making his selections from the opposite political party and indicates what can be achieved under the appointive system if the bar and the public are alert and interested. England clearly demonstrates that a tradition of nonpartisan appointment can be established, although the special factor of the existence of the barrister class and the limitation of appointments to that class present a situation which is not strictly comparable with that in the United States. Many good judges are selected in all countries and in the various states no matter what system of selection is employed—appointive, legislative vote, popular election, career judiciary, or a combination of these methods. The problem is to employ that method or methods which will consistently achieve the selection of the best judges in a given jurisdiction. The most appropriate method for the selection of appellate judges may not be the most suitable method for the choice of the numerous necessary trial judges.[84] The selective process can be made easier if after thorough objective and nonpartisan study some basic qualifications as to the requisite education and experiences necessary for judicial office can be established. Admission to the bar is basic. But thorough examination of the careers of eminent jurists and of the demands of the judicial office is necessary to determine what other requirements should be made. Promotion in the ranks, although not considered a desirable feature in England and although subject to abuse on the Continent, may have beneficial effects here. The judicial office requires an expertise which is secured in England by restricting appointments to the barrister class, and on the Continent to the judicial profession. Some methods or requirements may be necessary in the United States for the development of a specialist group from among the legal profession as a whole, whose experience and training will make them better judicial material.

No method of selection is foolproof. No system could be worse, how-

---

JUDGES 238-284 (1944). For an appraisal of the conduct of judges, see VANDERBILT, MINIMUM STANDARDS OF JUDICIAL ADMINISTRATION 12-16 (1949). Note also observations in CARPENTER, JUDICIAL TENURE IN THE UNITED STATES 211-212 (1917); HUGHES, THE SUPREME COURT OF THE UNITED STATES 17 (1928).

[84] Cf. interesting suggestion that inferior federal court judges be appointed by the chief justice with the approval of the supreme court in order to eliminate political appointments. Shartel, *Federal Judges—Appointment, Supervision and Removal*, 28 MICH. L. REV. 485 (1930). Note also the distinction practiced in Japan where supreme court judges are appointed by the cabinet and must go before the people at ten-year intervals while the inferior court judges having the requisite training and experience are appointed by the cabinet upon nomination by the supreme court. Oppler, *The Reform of Japan's Legal and Judicial System Under Allied Occupation*, 24 WASH. L. REV. 290, 309-312 (1949).

ever, than popular election on the party ticket along with a host of other national, state and local party candidates running for a variety of offices especially in cosmopolitan areas. In such circumstances there is not the slightest chance of a judge being thus selected on the basis of his qualifications for the office.[85] As we have seen, many desirable potential judges who would accept an appointment to the bench are disinclined to encounter the recurring hazards of a political campaign for election and so the field of choice is unfortunately narrowed. Our lack of definite knowledge as to what makes a good judge makes the problem difficult. Although the practice of executive appointment from among leading barristers has produced excellent results in England, even there every now and then a distinguished barrister proves to be a mediocre judge. Moreover, in practice in the United States, appointments to the bench have too often been treated purely as political patronage. The appointive system has its virtues in that responsibility is fixed on one person or in a group and is preferable to the elective system. If the bar and the public are alert to the importance of good judges, the appointing power is necessarily inclined to attempt to secure competent personnel within party limits, since he will be identified with the appointments and as an agent of the people is subject to popular control. The respect accorded the federal bench and its prestige generally lends support to those who favor the appointive system. Experience shows that appointed judges are more liberal than elected judges and are actually more aware of and responsive to current popular desires.[86] But good judges are not to be expected under any system in this country without the cooperation of the bar and the public.

There is much to be said for requiring, under any plan, the appointment of all judges on a bipartisan basis. Justice, on principle, should be bipartisan. Its administration should not be vested in a single party. Bipartisan appointments are the best way of proving to the public that one party does not control the courts and that the courts are not in

---

[85] Prof. Harold Laski, the British Laborite and a serious student of American institutions, strongly condemned the elective system for selecting judges. *The Technique of Judicial Appointment,* 24 MICH. L. REV. 529, 531, 532 (1926) stated: "For the election of judges by popular vote there is nothing to be said. Insofar as its underlying assumption is the belief that the people should choose those by whom they are to be governed it omits to note the vital fact that the qualifications for judicial office are not such as an undifferentiated public can properly assess.... Knowledge of the law, the balanced mind, the ability to brush aside unessentials and drive to the heart of a case—that a candidate will possess these qualities can, at best, be known only to a few. The people do not, in fact, choose their judges, they decide between the candidates of opposing parties. . . . The method of election, if it is for a short term, means insecurity of tenure; and that position is fatal to a proper judicial habit of mind. . . ."

[86] *E.g.,* HAYNES, *op. cit. supra* n. 83 at 184-216. See also CARPENTER, *op. cit. supra* n. 83 at 211-215.

politics.[87] The matter is of especial importance in the decision of highly controversial political issues. If all the judges in a bipartisan court, regardless of party affiliations, concur in the decision of such an issue, as they frequently do, their decision carries a weight with the public that an opinion from a partisan bench could not possibly do.

While the legal profession and the judges themselves have gradually realized the need for the judiciary to divorce themselves from political matters, this has proved to be difficult to attain. Although the role of partisan politics in the selection of judges and in pressures on the judiciary is deplorable this does not mean that prior political activities should disqualify a person for judicial office. In many ways experience in politics and in other branches of government is most useful to widen the horizons of a lawyer. But continued political activity by judges is another matter. And yet where judges must seek reelection political interferences and influences and participation in politics by judges who may only wish to continue in office must be anticipated.

While at times some have questioned whether the judiciary should be independent of popular control in a democracy, the need of such independence seems self evident for the protection of individual and minority rights. The importance of the impartial enforcement of the law means that the judiciary should not be subject to any pressures, even those of the people. In the end, if basic constitutional rights are to be maintained, faith must be placed in some group and the American way has been to entrust this duty to the judiciary. The common law tradition of independence has resulted by and large in good judges being the usual matter and exceptions being rare especially at the higher levels.

As Chief Justice White so deftly said in an era not given to frank speech concerning the judiciary:

> "Indeed, as I look at the subject, and contemplate the varied methods by which judges have been selected, the frequent shortness of their tenure, the almost usual inadequacy of their compensation, the natural exultation and pride in our profession which comes to me is tempered by a sense of reverent restraint, since the thought cannot be resisted that a result so remarkable has been brought about by the dispensation of a Merciful Providence in vouchsafing the fulfillment of the promise, 'As thy days, so shall thy strength be.' "[88]

One may doubt the wisdom of depending upon a "Merciful Providence" in matters in which we have the power as well as the duty to safeguard the courts and all whom they serve from undesirable judicial appointments.

---

[87] See Canon 2 of the CANONS OF PROFESSIONAL ETHICS OF THE AMERICAN BAR ASSOCIATION as to the duties of the profession in eliminating partisan consideration from judicial selection.

[88] 7 A.B.A.J. 341.

## III

### The Functions, Qualifications and Selection of Jurors

#### 1. The Functions of Jurors

The jury[1] is undoubtedly the institution that most distinguishes trials at common law from trials under the Roman law, where a jury was unknown. It is only in those portions of our law that were imported from the Continent—equity, probate and admiralty matters that followed in large degree the civil procedure of the Continent—that a jury is not used.[2] It is the jury that gives English and American trials their distinctive characteristics.

As a substitute for the earlier modes of trial—trial by ordeal, trial by battle and wager of law—trial by jury was as daring an innovation as has ever been attempted in the history of the common law.[3] The origin of the jury may be traced back to the ninth century and the usages of the Carolingian monarchs from whom it was taken over by the Normans and thence transferred to England. The English gradually developed it as a mode of trial which first was made available in the royal common law courts alone for certain types of action; indeed, this more rational mode of trial was one of the prime reasons for the growing popularity of the royal courts.

The jury was originally a group of neighbors whose testimony was solicited as to their knowledge of the facts of an occurrence or of the ownership or possession of land. As dwellers in the locality, the jurors on the basis of personal information would give the answers as to such matters. "They are not judges . . . their function is . . . 'to recognize, to speak the truth.' "[4] Not all residents of the vicinity were eligible as jurors, but from the first a property qualification was insisted upon. By the thirteenth century trial by jury was used in all criminal cases to determine the question of guilt or innocence and gradually trial by

---

[1] An investigation of the jury system is currently being conducted at the University of Chicago Law School. See Meltzer, *A Projected Study of the Jury as a Working Institution*, 287 ANNALS 97 (1953) for a delimitation of the areas to be studied.

[2] Since generally there no longer is a separation into law and equity courts, the question of the availability of a jury trial depends on whether the action was formerly at law because of the frequent constitutional provisions preserving the common law right to a jury trial. *E.g.* U.S. CONST. Art. III, sec. 2; Amend. VI, VII; FED. R. CIV. P. 38, 39; FED. R. CRIM. P. 23, see Note, *The Right to Jury Trial Under Merged Procedure*, 65 HARV. L. REV. 453 (1952).

[3] See MAITLAND, THE FORMS OF ACTION AT COMMON LAW 18-19 (1936); MILLAR, CIVIL PROCEDURE OF THE TRIAL COURT IN HISTORICAL PERSPECTIVE 17-23 (1952).

[4] 2 POLLOCK & MAITLAND, HISTORY OF ENGLISH LAW 629 (2d ed. 1898). Thus also, GLANVILLE, THE LAWS AND CUSTOMS OF ENGLAND, 53 (Beames ed. 1900): "If none of them (the jurors) are acquainted with the truth of the matter, and this be testified upon their oaths in Court, recourse must be had to others, until such can be found who do know the truth of it."

jury was extended to almost every kind of civil action. And by 1600 the jury was the usual mode of trial in the common law courts in all cases except for some of the extraordinary legal remedies such as certiorari, mandamus and the like. Although at that time their character as witnesses basing their verdict on their own knowledge of the facts was not completely forgotten, testimony was being presented to the jurors for their consideration in deciding the issues. It was not for more than another century that it became established that the jurors, instead of giving a verdict based on their own knowledge, were to form an impartial body, having no opinion as to the case at issue and limited to deciding the case on the basis of the evidence presented in court.[5]

Highly valued as the petit jury was by the parties to a civil suit or by a defendant in a criminal proceeding, it was the grand jury that was popularly—and correctly—deemed the essence of an Englishman's liberty. The grand jury, which alone could indict persons suspected of crime, dates back at least to 1166.[6] It was deemed the individual's greatest protection against attempts on his life and liberty in the centuries when absolute monarchs on the Continent did not hesitate to interfere with a subject's freedom by imprisoning him without warrant or trial or even to grant *lettres de cachet* giving favorites similar privileges over their enemies. While we may not pause to consider at length the ramifications of the operation of the grand jury, we must note that it was preserved in the Fifth Amendment to the Federal Constitution and also in many state constitutions.[7]

The trial jury likewise became in some degree a shield in the trial of both civil and criminal cases not only against the harsh rules of the

---

[5] See Mylock v. Saladine, 1 Bl. W. 481, 96 Eng. Rep. 278 (K.B. 1764) in which Lord Mansfield said: "I have no doubt of the propriety of changing the venue, where an indifferent trial cannot be had, nor of the power of this Court to change it, when such a case appears. A juror should be as a white paper, and know neither plaintiff nor defendant, but judge of the issue merely as an abstract proposition upon the evidence presented before him. He should be superior even to a suspicion of partiality. . . ."
See for history of the English development of the jury, 1 HOLDSWORTH, HISTORY OF ENGLISH LAW 312-350 (5th ed. 1931).

[6] 1 POLLOCK & MAITLAND, *op. cit. supra* n. 4 at 151-152; Hornard, *The Jury of Presentment and the Assize of Clarenden*, 56 ENG. HIST. REV. 374 (1941). For general discussion and an appraisal of the functions of the grand jury see ORFIELD, CRIMINAL PROCEDURE FROM ARREST TO APPEAL 135-193 (1947).

[7] In spite of the more frequent use of the information today, ORFIELD, *op. cit. supra* n. 6 at 144, 209-214, and the observation "that grand juries as they function in the United States today tend to rubberstamp the recommendations of prosecuting attorneys", so careful a student of these matters as Senator Wayne Morse, then Director of the Oregon Survey of the Administration of Criminal Justice, concluded that "The grand jury can be an effective instrument for the investigation of political fraud and corruption and does serve as a constant warning to public officials that they cannot escape public scrutiny." *A Survey of the Grand Jury System*, 10 ORE. L. REV. 101, 217, 295 (1931) at 306 and 363. To a similar effect as to the possible effective use of the grand jury see DIENSTEIN, ARE YOU GUILTY? 100-101 (1954).

early common law but also against the more than occasional overbearing or subservient judge, for, as we have seen, up to the time of the Act of Settlement of 1701, judges merely served at the king's pleasure instead of during good behavior and a litigant had to fear that a judge might be more responsive to the royal will rather than to justice. Since at common law the jurors all had to agree to a verdict, a single juror might and often has mitigated the strict operation of the common law or some statute. On the other hand, it may be added, a single juror may and often has obstructed justice.[8]

At first the only recourse against the verdict of a trial jury was by the verdict of another jury—a jury of twenty-four—that the first had perjured itself. This remedy, the writ of attaint, which developed while the jurors were still considered as witnesses rather than judges of the facts, resulted in the reversal of the first verdict and the imposition of very severe penalties on the original jury.[9] The difficulties in obtaining a second verdict and the gradual change in the character of the jury made the remedy less effective. The Tudors and Stuarts employed the Council and Star Chamber to exercise pressure on juries by punishing them for corruption or false verdicts, and verdicts contrary to the Star Chamber's view of the evidence were likely to be considered corrupt or false.

It was not until 1670 in the famous *Bushell's Case*[10] that jurors were really rendered free to determine their verdict without liability even if contrary to the court's direction. *Bushell's Case* did for the jury what the Act of Settlement at a later date, as we have seen, did for the judges—it gave them independence. This decision concerned the jurors who had acquitted two Quakers (one of them William Penn) in spite of the court's having attempted to extract a different verdict by keeping them without meat and drink for three days. For their conduct the jurors were fined and imprisoned. On a writ of habeas corpus they were discharged, Chief Justice Vaughan rendering a notable opinion in which he distinguished between the ministerial acts and the judicial acts of the jury; "the verdict itself, when given, is not an act ministerial but judicial, and according to the best of their judgment, for which they

---

[8] HALE, HISTORY OF THE COMMON LAW 293 (4th ed., 1792) testifying as to the value of unanimity, stated: "this gives a great weight, value and credit to such a verdict, wherein twelve men must unanimously agree in a matter of FACT, and none dissent; though it must be agreed, that an ignorant parcel of men are sometimes governed by a few that are more knowing, or of greater interest, or reputation than the rest."

[9] 1 HOLDSWORTH, *op. cit. supra* n. 5 at 337-347; 2 POLLOCK & MAITLAND, *op. cit. supra* n. 4 at 541-542, 665. GLANVILLE, *op. cit. supra* n. 4 at 56, details the punishment of members of the grand assize who perjured themselves.

[10] 6 How. St. Tr. 999, Vaug. Rep. 135, 124 Eng. Rep. 1006 (C.P. 1670).

are not finable nor to be punished, but by attaint."[11] The court reasoned that the jury are the judges of the facts. If a judge can order the jury on pain of punishment to take his view of the facts, what is the use of the jury? As the jury are judges of the facts, a disagreement with the judge as to the findings of fact cannot be penal:

> "Without a fact agreed, it is as impossible for a Judge, or any other, to know the law relating to that fact, or direct concerning it, as to know an accident that hath no subject.
>
> "Hence it follows, that the Judge can never direct what the law is in any matter controverted, without first knowing the fact; and then it follows, that without his previous knowledge of the fact, the jury cannot go against his direction in law, for he could not direct. . . .
>
> "But upon all general issues . . . (the jury) find for the plaintiff or defendant upon the issue to be tryed, wherein they resolve both law and fact complicately, and not the fact by itself; so though they answer not singly to the question what is the law, yet they determine the law in all matters where issue is joyn'd and tryed in the principal case, but where the verdict is special."[12]

Gradually attaint for a false verdict fell into disuse. As juries could no longer be penalized for finding a verdict contrary to judicial direction, the only way in which the crown could exert pressure was by controlling the choice of the jury, a practice which the Stuarts did not hesitate to exercise.[13] Such evil practices, however, came to an end with the Revolution. The legitimate way of controlling erroneous verdicts came to be by an order, after a hearing, setting aside the verdict and directing a new trial.

The function of the jurors[14] from the first was confined to dealing with facts. Questions of law were for the court. This division of responsibility between the judge and the jury did much to determine the nature of the pleadings at common law,[15] molded the rules of evidence, and influenced trial procedure generally. Inasmuch as the jury were laymen, not versed in court procedure, the essential aim of common-law pleadings, in which the parties to a suit stated alternately their rival contentions, was to bring the pleadings to a point where the respective parties took opposite positions on some relevant question of law or fact.

---

[11] 6 How. St. Tr. at 1019, Vaug. Rep. at 152, 124 Eng. Rep. at 1014. For details of William Penn's Trial see 6 How. St. Tr. 951 (1670).
[12] 6 How. St. Tr. at 1010, 1014-17, Vaug. Rep. at 147, 150, 124 Eng. Rep. at 1012, 1013.
[13] See Havighurst, *The Judiciary and Politics in the Reign of Charles II*, 66 L.Q. REV. 229, 241-244 (1950).
[14] See generally, Broeder, *The Functions of the Jury: Fact or Fiction*, 21 U. CHI. L. REV. 386 (1954).
[15] See Holdsworth, *The Development of Oral and Written Pleadings*, 2 SELECT ESSAYS IN ANGLO-AMERICAN LEGAL HISTORY 614, 619-626 (1908).

If they disagreed on a question of law, the court would dispose of the question of law on a demurrer. But if they disagreed on a relevant question of fact, an issue of fact was raised for a trial by jury. The great objective in a jury trial was thus the determination of a *single* question of fact. In this way it was hoped, and with a considerable measure of success, to submit to the jury an issue which was simple and entirely within their competence and to prevent misleading contentions on a variety of matters from beclouding their thinking. Even with these limitations it was deemed essential that the jury work under the supervision of the trial judge, who was to confine the activities of counsel to its proper sphere. The trial judge would prevent counsel from straying beyond the proper bounds of the case in their respective opening addresses to the jury, in offering documents and in presenting the oral testimony of witnesses by appropriate rulings of law, when objections were raised by counsel, on the evidence and by his concluding charge on the law to the jury. At common law the judge might question the witnesses where necessary in his opinion to bring out all the truth, and in delivering his charge he might analyze the evidence, summarize it and comment on it so long as he made it very clear that the resolution of the issue of the fact is exclusively the province of the jury.

Two further observations should be made on the course of a trial by jury. First, if the meaning of a written instrument is drawn into issue at common law, its meaning is to be determined by the court, for the reason that in the early days and until recently in some jurisdictions, at least, there were jurors who could not read and accordingly there was nobody but the judge left to determine the factual issue of the meaning of the document. Secondly, in recent times greater liberality has been permitted under modern procedure in allowing more than one question of fact to go to the jury and in the consolidation for trial of two or more cases arising out of the same transaction or involving common questions of law and fact. Such has been the progress of popular education that these changes in jury trials work no injustice and prevent a multiplicity of trials, where the judge retains his common-law powers of supervising the trial and where he is a competent, alert judge, but where the trial judge has been stripped by statute of his common-law powers or is incompetent or weak, much injustice can and is being done in modern complicated trials because of confusion of the jury.

As the seventeenth century developments indicate, the jury trial as conducted in England was still primitive in many essentials when the American colonies were first established and even well into the eighteenth century. Since the jurors were only beginning to be recognized as judges of the evidence rather than as witnesses, the devices for judicial guidance of the jurors in the proper performance of their function, which had not been essential earlier, were just originating. It was this primitive uncontrolled form of the jury trial which was transplanted to America. In this period because of the oppressive action of many of the Stuart judges and the few outstanding samples of a jury refusing to knuckle under to such judges[16] and because of the tendency of the commonly non-professional colonial crown-appointed judges to favor the crown in colonial disputes, there was an increasing inclination to place reliance on the decision of the jurors.[17] Juries were popular in America as communal representatives in a day when the battle cry was "No taxation without representation." As a result, both federal and state constitutions embodied provisions insuring the right to trial by jury.[18]

The essential elements of the common law trial by jury embodied in the federal constitution have been recognized to be: "(1) that the jury

---

[16] *E.g.* The famous trial of William Penn, 6 How. St. Tr. 951 (1670) and that of Peter Zenger, 17 How. St. Tr. 675 (1735).

[17] See POUND, CRIMINAL JUSTICE IN AMERICA 115 (1945). In the Province of West Jersey a law of 1681 provided that 12 men of the neighborhood sat with the three justices to hear all cases, the justices merely to assist the jurors in questions of law and to pronounce the judgment of the jurors "in whom only the judgment resides." LEAMING & SPICER, GRANTS, CONCESSIONS AND ORIGINAL CONSTITUTION OF THE PROVINCE OF NEW JERSEY 426-428 (2d ed. 1881, originally printed 1752). Note observation of TANNER, THE PROVINCE OF NEW JERSEY, 1664-1738, 480-484 (1908), that no jury ever convicted defendants tried for contempt of the government in actions instituted by the Governor in an attempt to intimidate and control the colonists. The Governor also was unable to secure indictments from the grand jury for alleged seditious words criticizing him and so was forced to act via informations.

Thus also Andrew Hamilton's speech to the jury in the Trial of John Peter Zenger, 17 How. St. Tr. 675 (1735) (reprinted from Zenger's account in 1813):

"Then, gentlemen of the jury, it is to you we must now appeal, for witnesses to the truth of the facts we have offered, and are denied the liberty to prove . . . were you to find a verdict against my client, you must take upon you to say, the papers referred to in the information, and which we acknowledge we printed and published, are false, scandalous, and seditious; but of this I can have no apprehension. . . . I know they (the jury) have the right, beyond all dispute, to determine both the law and the fact; and where they do not doubt of the law, they ought to do so. This of leaving it to the judgment of the Court, whether the words are libellous or not, in effect renders juries useless (to say no worse) in many cases. . . . The right of the jury to find such a verdict as they in their conscience do think is agreeable to their evidence, is supported by the authority of Bushell's case . . . (I insist) it is very plain, that the jury are by law at liberty . . . to find both the law and the fact. . . ." At 703, 706, 716.

[18] The federal constitution originally included only the provision as to jury trial in criminal cases. U.S. CONST. Art. III sec. 2. Because of widespread popular feeling, extensions of the provisions for jury trial were included in the first ten amendments. U.S. CONST. Amend. VI, VII. Cf. discussion in The Federalist, No. 83 (Hamilton), as to the diversity of jury trial usage among the original thirteen states, noting that: ". . . it is evident that though trial by jury, with various limitations, is known to each state individually, yet in the United States, *as such,* it is at this time altogether unknown because the present federal government has no judiciary power whatever."

should consist of twelve men, neither more nor less; (2) that the trial should be in the presence and under the superintendence of a judge having power to instruct them as to the law and advise them in respect of the facts; and (3) that the verdict should be unanimous...."[19] The occurrences in the jury room are secret in the sense that no one other than a member of the jury may be present during its deliberations and a juror may not be compelled to testify to what happened therein. If, however, it is first shown that a juror in some way was disqualified from serving as a juror, the other jurors may give testimony in corroboration of such facts.[20]

We too often think of juries solely from the point of view of the litigants. It is interesting to have the view of a French judge who has written more understandingly of this country than has any other foreigner. Said Alexis De Tocqueville:

> "I do not know whether the jury is useful to those who have law suits; but I am certain it is highly beneficial to those who judge them; and I look upon it as one of the most efficacious means for the education of the people which society can employ."[21]

The jury is beneficial to the judge for at least two reasons. First of all, the facts of a case, both at the trial and appellate levels, are often more difficult to decide than the law of the case. Secondly and far more important, it spares him from making the harsh decisions that the sharp application of the law to the actual facts of a hard case would often require.[22] While on the one hand in some cases juries may flaunt the law, in many cases juries effect equity. That basically was why the American colonists complained in the Declaration of Independence of the king "depriving us in many cases of the benefits of trial by jury," referring particularly to the establishment in the colonies of admiralty courts.[23] Had the cases arising under the English trade acts been tried

---

[19] Patton v. United States, 281 U.S. 276, 288, 50 S.Ct. 253, 74 L.Ed. 854 (1930). As to the nonwaiver of unanimity in the federal courts see Hibdon v. United States, 204 F.2d 834 (6th Cir. 1953). 67 HARV. L. REV. 897 (1954). *Cf.* as to a state court, Minneapolis & St. Louis R.R. Co. v. Bombolis, 241 U.S. 211, 36 S.Ct. 595, 60 L.Ed. 961 (1916); see also MILLAR, *op. cit. supra*, n. 3 at 263-264.

[20] See Clark v. United States, 289 U.S. 1, 12-18, 53 S.Ct. 465, 77 L.Ed. 993 (1933).

[21] 1 Democracy in America 285 (Reeves text, Bowen rev., 1945). But cf. Broeder *supra* n. 14, at 21.

[22] See BOK, BACKBONE OF THE HERRING 195 (1941); POUND, THE TASK OF LAW 83-84 (1941); ULMAN, A JUDGE TAKES THE STAND 23 et seq. (1933); Wyzanski, *A Trial Judge's Freedom and Responsibility*, 65 HARV. L. REV. 1281 (1952). For criticism of the jury as judges of the law cf. Broeder, *supra* n. 14, at 401-413.

[23] DUMBAULD, THE DECLARATION OF INDEPENDENCE, WHAT IT MEANS TODAY 132-133 (1950). See also IV ANDREWS, COLONIAL PERIOD IN AMERICAN HISTORY, ENGLAND'S COMMERCIAL AND COLONIAL POLICY 222-271 (1938); WASHBURNE, IMPERIAL CONTROL OF THE ADMINISTRATION OF JUSTICE 164-177 (105 Col. U.

in the ordinary courts with a jury, probably there would have been no convictions. Accordingly the colonists felt aggrieved and much of this predilection for jury decision was to persist through the nineteenth century.[24]

In this country the unsettled state of the law after the Revolution and the fact that trained judges and lawyers were few in number led to increasing respect and reliance on the decision of jurors as representatives of the community giving judgment. Since many of the early judges did not have professional qualifications and could not claim a superior knowledge of the law, it is no wonder that they were distrusted and that jurors were accorded great powers. In the Jeffersonian and in the Jacksonian periods the use of jurors appealed to pioneer provincialism and the pressures of the intensified desires for democracy led to constitutional and statutory provisions and even judicial decisions in many of the states, making jurors judges of the law as well as of the fact either generally or at least in criminal prosecutions.[25] Indeed the enactment of popular but unconstitutional statutes led to a demand of some groups that the jury should pass on their constitutionality and enforceability. This movement in the first half of the nineteenth century to enlarge the powers of the jury was part and parcel of the movement we have previously described of restricting the powers of the trial judge[26] and the effect on the administration of justice was equally harmful. Nevertheless, we find that until 1895 federal judges sometimes instructed juries that they were the judges both of the law and the facts. It was not until *Sparfe & Hansen v. United States*[27] that the duty of the jury to follow the court's instructions as to the law was finally

---

Studies in Hist. Econ. & Pub. Law, No. 2, 1923); Pittman, *The Emancipated Judiciary in America: Its Colonial and Constitutional History*, 37 A.B.A.J. 485, 545 (1951).

[24] As Dean Pound has sagely remarked: "Jury lawlessness has been the great corrective of law in its actual administration. . . . A tendency to extend the scope of jury lawlessness, manifest in the last century in almost all American jurisdictions, indicates that there are many points where the law as it stood lacked social psychological guarantee." THE TASK OF LAW, 83 (1941).

[25] Howe, *Juries as Judges of Criminal Law*, 52 HARV. L. REV. 582 (1939) discusses "the judiciary's response to a specific demand of democratic theory—the demand that the jury in criminal cases should not only determine the facts but judge the law as well." As Professor Howe put it, after the decision in Bushell's case, discussed herein at p. 53, "The political question was immediately presented: if a criminal jury is not liable for any punishment when it disregards the court's instructions, then it possesses the power to determine for itself what the law may be. If it has the power, why has it not the right? . . . The conflict between democratic hopes and English common law traditions, between a frontier concept of popular justice and an old world fact of King's law, was sharply mirrored in the issue as to what limits were to be set to the jury's rights." At 583, 584.

[26] Lecture I at p. 6, ff.

[27] 156 U.S. 51, 15 S.Ct. 273, 39 L.Ed. 343 (1895). The majority and dissenting opinions in the case consider the leading American decisions relevant to this question. For comments on this decision see Broeder, *supra*, n. 14, 403-404.

established in the United States courts. By the latter part of the nineteenth century, as the legal profession grew and the bench became manned by trained lawyers in most states also, the jury was commonly limited to its original function of the decision of questions of facts and was held to be bound by the judge's instructions as to the law.[28]

Judge Story's statement of the common-law demarcation of the province of the jury, enunciated in 1835 finally came to prevail:

> "My opinion is, that the jury are no more judges of the law in a capital or other criminal case, upon the plea of not guilty, than they are in every civil case, tried upon the general issue. In each of these cases, their verdict, when general, is necessarily compounded of the law and of the fact; and includes both. In each they must necessarily determine the law, as well as the fact. In each, they have the physical power to disregard the law, as laid down to them by the court. But I deny, that, in any case, civil or criminal, they have the moral right to decide the law according to their own notions, or pleasure. On the contrary, I hold it the most sacred constitutional right of every party accused of a crime, that the jury should respond as to the facts, and the court as to the law. It is the duty of the court to instruct the jury as to the law; and it is the duty of the jury to follow the law, as it is laid down by the court. This is the right of every citizen; and it is his only protection. If the jury were at liberty to settle the law for themselves, the effect would be, not only that the law itself would be most uncertain, from the different views, which the different juries might take of it; but in case of error there would be no remedy or redress by the injured party; for the court would not have the right to review the law as it had been settled by the jury."[29]

As previously has been said, at the same time that juries were frequently declared the judges of law as well as the facts of litigation, the judges' powers to instruct the jury orally as to the law, or to analyze, summarize or comment on the evidence were often restricted. Although in many of the state courts the jury ostensibly no longer has the freedom to decide the law it formerly had, where it still must function without the guidance of the trial judge[30] it undoubtedly decides much law. As Professor Sunderland said:

> "The peculiarity of the general verdict is the merger into a single individual *residuum* of all matters, however numerous, whether of law or fact. It is a compound made by the jury which is incapable

---

[28] As to the gradual limitation of the jury's freedom of decision see Howe, *supra*, n. 25. Juries are still supposedly judges of the law and facts in three states: GA. CONST. sec. 2, par. 1; IND. CONST. Art. I, sec. 19; MD. CONST. Art. 15, sec. 5. Even in these states the constitutional provisions have been limited in their application. Howe, *supra* n. 25, at 597, n. 58, at 614, n. 125, 126.

[29] United States v. Battiste, 24 Fed. Case 1042, 1043, No. 15, 545 (C.C.D. Mass. 1835).

[30] See Lecture I, herein at p. 6, ff. as to this development.

of being broken up into its constituent parts.... The general verdict is as inscrutable and essentially mysterious as the judgment which issued from the ancient oracles of Delphi. Both stood on the same foundation—a presumption of wisdom."[31]

This American practice is in sharp contrast with developments in England. There as jurors were recognized to be judging the evidence proferred at the trial, they were subjected to judicial direction as to the weight of the evidence and as to the pertinent law and their function was clearly delimited. As Holdsworth has said:

"The jury works well in England mainly because the bench is stronger than the bar . . . its success is due to the same causes as those to which the development and the success of our system of case law are due . . . the jurors . . . are, in the habit of looking to the summing up by the judge for guidance, rather than to the orations of counsel. Thus the bench is able to assert its prerogative as the judge of the law, and the jury's prerogative as judge of the fact; and to prevent both from being infringed."[32]

The contrast between English and American jury practice[33] is not to our credit. The American Bar Association has taken the lead in recommending that:

"After the evidence has been closed and counsel have concluded their arguments to the jury, the trial judge should instruct the jury orally as to the law of the case and should have the power to advise them as to the facts by summarizing and analyzing the evidence and commenting upon the weight and credibility of the evidence or upon any part of it, always leaving the final decision on questions of fact to the jury."[34]

---

[31] Sunderland, *Verdicts, General and Special*, 29 YALE L.J. 253, 258 (1920).

[32] SOME LESSONS FROM OUR LEGAL HISTORY 85 (1928). As to the judge's function in jury cases in England see JOWITT, THE STRANGE CASE OF ALGER HISS (1953) 150-151. For an example of judicial comment at a contemporary trial in England see TRIAL OF CHRISTOPHER CRAIG AND DEREK WILLIAM BENTLEY (Hyde ed. 1952), 195, 197, 199-204. Lord Chief Justice Goddard observed inter alia after describing Craig's action in firing and reloading the revolver: "If that is not a deliberate act, a deliberate firing, it is difficult to understand what would be" (199-200). In discussing whether Craig knew Bentley was armed he stated further: "You are not bound to believe Bentley if you think the inference and common sense of the matter overwhelming that he must have known he had it." (at 203). Lord Goddard after mentioning the police testimony queried, "Are you going to say they (the police) are conspicuous liars? . . . Do you believe that those three officers have come into the box and sworn what is deliberately untrue? Those three officers who on that night showed a devotion to duty for which they are entitled to the thanks of the community?" At 204.

[33] See for details of present American practice, Wright, *The Invasion of Jury: Temperature of the War*, 27 TEMP. L.Q. 137 (1953); *Instructions to the Jury: Summary Without Comment*, 1954, WASH. U.L.Q. 177. The differences between the English and American practice even in those states where comments on the evidence are permissible are detailed in the latter article.

[34] 63 A.B.A. REP. 523 (1938). See VANDERBILT, MINIMUM STANDARDS OF JUDICIAL ADMINISTRATION, 536-538, 224-234 (1949). See for similar recommendations of committee of experts for the COMMONWEALTH FUND, MORGAN, CHAFEE,

## JUDGES AND JURORS

The problem of the juror's function today has various facets. The question of the demarcation of questions of fact for jury's decision from the question of law for judicial decision continues to cause trouble because of the many instances where the decisions of questions of fact necessarily have legal connotations. In one view the basic problem is to so control the jury as to limit it to its function of deciding issues of fact. In the view of many the special verdict and special interrogatories are useful devices to serve this purpose.[35] On the other hand there are others who testify to the value of the jury as an expression of community opinion.[36] Despite the general acceptance of the proposition that questions of law are for the court and questions of fact only are for the jury, the jury's power to decide the whole case by a general verdict, frequently without the guidance of the judge to decide issues of law, is the crux of the dispute. The conflict is between those, on the one hand, who would limit the freedom of the jury by proper instructions by the judge, his comments on the evidence, use of his power to withdraw the case from the jury when the evidence is insufficient,[37] as well as by devices such as the special verdict, and those, on the other hand, who regard this freedom of the jury to decide the law in some cases in the guise of a general verdict as a welcome power.[38] It is said by the latter that "Traditionally juries are the devices by which the rigor of the law is modified pending the enactment of new statutes."[39]

---

GIFFORD, HINTON, HOUGH, JOHNSTON, SUNDERLAND, WIGMORE, THE LAW OF EVIDENCE, SOME PROPOSALS FOR ITS REFORM (1927) 9, 21. The American Law Institute's MODEL CODE OF EVIDENCE (1942) embodies a similar proposition as Rule 8. See Lecture I herein at p. 5.

[35] As to the use of special verdicts and the recommendations of the American Bar Association as to their use see VANDERBILT, *op. cit. supra* n. 34 at 237-243, 540. FED. R. CIV. P. 49 authorizes special verdicts and special interrogatories. See Driver, *A Consideration of the More Extended Use of the Special Verdict*, 25 WASH. L. REV. 45 (1950); Sunderland, *supra* n. 31. See also full discussion in in Judge Jerome Frank's opinion in Skidmore v. Baltimore & O. R. Co., 167 F.2d 54 (2d Cir. 1948). It is to be noted that Judge Frank is very critical of the jury. See FRANK, LAW AND THE MODERN MIND 170-185 (1930); COURTS ON TRIAL 108-125 (1949).

[36] See authorities cited in n. 22 *supra*.

[37] See Rhodes v. Metropolitan Life Ins. Co., 172 F.2d 183 (5th Cir. 1949) cert. den. 337 U.S. 930; Comment, *Federal Courts, Directed Verdicts in Civil Actions*, 47 MICH. L. REV. 974 (1949). As to the withdrawal of a case from jury consideration on a motion for directed verdict and the constitutional guaranties of a jury trial, see majority and dissenting opinions in Galloway v. United States, 319 U.S. 372, 63 S.Ct. 1077, 87 L.Ed. 1458, rehearing den., 320 U.S. 214, 63 S.Ct. 1442, 87 L.Ed. 1851 (1943).

[38] See Wyzanski, *A Trial Judge's Freedom and Responsibility*, 65 HARV. L. REV. 1281 (1952) indicating cases in which a trial judge's comments on the evidence should be restricted. Cf. James, *Functions of Judge and Jury in Negligence Cases*, 58 YALE L.J. 667 (1949). The author concludes that "Any rule of substantive law or procedure which enlarges the jury's theoretical sphere tends to extend liability, and conversely, any rule which restricts the jury's sphere tends to restrict liability." At 689.

[39] Wyzanski, *supra*, n. 38, at 1286. Thus also Dean Pound has said: "At common law the chief reliance for individualizing the application of law is the power

Others are more critical of the jury making "its own 'law' in each case with little or no knowledge of, or reference to, what has been done before or regard to what will be done thereafter in similar cases."[40] In such view prejudice is "the thirteenth juror."[41]

Although the jury is used to a decreasing extent even in the United States, the constitutional guarantees of trial by jury insure that so long as the parties so desire they shall have the jury to which they are entitled. Trial by jury is a vital feature of judicial administration in this country, but the jury's lack of information as to the law and its lack of experience in weighing the probative force of testimony makes the assistance and guidance of the judge whose only aim is to see that justice is done most essential. Since the judge may set aside a verdict and grant a new trial if the jury's verdict is opposed to the evidence, and may direct a verdict if there is no evidence to support any but one verdict, it is only logical that the jury be guided by the judge's analysis, summary and comments on the evidence. The importance of a proper allocation of powers and functions between the judge and the jury is essential to the continued and proper employment of the trial jury.[42]

## 2. *Qualifications of Jurors*

Originally jurors were neighbors who had certain property qualifications, "otherwise they shall not be sworn, lest through their hunger and poverty they may be easily corrupted or suborned."[43]

In England even today

"A juror must be (1) a £10 freeholder, or (2) a £20 long leaseholder, or (3) a householder in the valuation list of £30 in London and Middlesex or £20 elsewhere, or (4) occupy a house with not less than fifteen windows."[44]

Inasmuch as more men occupy property than women, most of the jurors are men, and other adults, men or women, residing there are excluded from the jury list. Another result of the property requirement is that juries are largely confined to the English middle or upper classes so

---

of juries to render general verdicts, the power to find the facts in such a way as to compel a different result from that which the legal rule strictly applied would require. . . ." AN INTRODUCTION TO THE PHILOSOPHY OF LAW 65-66 (rev. ed. 1954).

[40] FRANK, COURTS ON TRIAL 120 (1949).

[41] *Id.* at 122. See accounts of attempts to discover some of the secrets of jury deliberations, Hervey, *The Jurors Look at Judges,* 18 OKLA. B.A.J. 1508 (1947); Hoffman & Brodley, *Jurors on Trial,* 17 Mo. L. REV. 235 (1952); Moffat, *As Jurors See a Law Suit,* 24 ORE. L. REV. 199 (1945); Wanamaker, *Trial by Jury,* 11 U. CIN. L. REV. 191 (1937).

[42] See Newman, *Should Jury Trials be Modernized,* 29 N. DAK. L. REV. 365 (1953).

[43] FORTESCUE, DE LAUDIBUS DE LEGUM ANGLIE, c. xxv at 59 (Chrimes ed. 1942).

[44] JACKSON, THE MACHINERY OF JUSTICE IN ENGLAND 240 (2d ed. 1953).

that it "is only by some stretch of the imagination that a working-class prisoner can be said to be tried by 'twelve representatives of his countrymen'."[45] Until 1949 there were also special jurors in England and special juries could be ordered in all civil or criminal cases other than treason or felony. Jury service in England is compulsory and failure to attend except for good cause leads to the imposition of a fine. Until recently jurors were unpaid, in many instances occasioning considerable hardship. Since 1949 all persons who attend for jury service are entitled to travelling and subsistence allowances and also to be compensated for loss of earnings or for additional expense incurred, not exceeding $1.40 for four hours' service, or $2.80 for a longer period in one day.[46]

From a group of propertied neighbors who were sworn to testify to the facts peculiarly within their knowledge to a group of impartial judges deciding on the testimony of others is a far cry indeed, but the Anglo-American jury was thus transformed from the twelfth to the twentieth centuries. In this day in which the organs of communication are far-reaching and widespread, publicity relating to the courts and particularly concerning criminal trials of violence, fraud against the government or treason, reach the public daily, the difficulty of satisfying the constitutional requirement of impartial jurors who have not prejudged the case before them is obvious.[47] The importance in obtaining an impartial jury of the qualification and exemption provided by law and the mode or selection of the jury is equally apparent.

The Supreme Court has said:

"The American tradition of trial by jury, considered in connection with either criminal or civil proceedings, necessarily contemplates an impartial jury drawn from a cross-section of the community.... This does not mean, of course, that every jury must contain representatives of all the economic, social, religious, racial, political and geographical groups of the community; frequently such complete representation would be impossible. But it does mean that the prospective jurors shall be selected by court officials without systematic and intentional exclusion of any of the groups. Recognition must be given to the fact that those eligible for jury service are to be found in every stratum of society. Jury competence is an individual rather than a group or class matter."[48]

---

[45] *Id.* at 241.
[46] *Id.* at 65, 240-243.
[47] In addition to attempts to eliminate biased jurors on the *voir dire* considered at Lecture III, pp. 72-74, changes of venue or continuances may be allowed to lessen the effects of prejudicial publicity. United States v. Florio, 13 F.R.D. 296 (S.D.N.Y. 1952) (change of venue); Delaney v. United States, 199 F.2d 107 (1st Cir. 1952) (continuance) but see United States v. Moran, 194 F.2d 623 (2d Cir. 1952) cert. den. 343 U.S. 965 (continuance refused, no change of venue requested). See also Notes, 53 COLUM. L. REV. 651 (1953), 63 HARV. L. REV. 846 (1950).
[48] Mr. Justice Murphy speaking for the Court in Thiel v. Southern Pac. Ry.

The Supreme Court's position as to the standards of jury selection applicable in federal courts was predicated not only on constitutional provisions, but more particularly on its position as the head of the federal court system, charged with supervision of the administration of justice in the federal courts.[49] Accordingly, in cases where juries in federal courts were involved, it has been considered that proof of prejudice to the defendant because of exclusion of a particular group was not required,[50] whereas when the composition of juries in state courts was questioned, the issue was the narrow one of constitutionality alone and proof of prejudice to the defendant by discrimination in the exclusion of particular classes was considered necessary.[51]

Like every other part of our judicial machinery, the jury requires intensive study looking to its better adaptation to present-day needs.[52] Here as in so many other phases of judicial administration the federal courts have led the way, largely through the work of a committee of district court judges in 1942 headed by Chief Judge John C. Knox of the United States District Court for the Southern District of New York under the direction of the Judicial Conference of the United States. The most thoroughgoing study of the jury in the state courts is that of the Committee on the Selection of Jurors of the Section of Judicial Administration of the American Bar Association.[53] Both reports agree with respect to the shortcomings of the jury system and in the main on the remedies to overcome such defects, but more progress has been made in rectifying conditions in the federal courts than in the states, though there is still room for improvement in the federal field.

What standards should govern the jury commissioners in appraising the qualifications of prospective jurymen? Strangely enough, there are

---

Co., 328 U.S. 217 at 220, 66 S.Ct. 984, 90 L.Ed. 1181 (1946), 35 Calif. L. Rev. 142, 59 Harv. L. Rev. 1167, 20 Temp. L.Q. 154 (1947). In this case the names of all persons who worked for a daily wage were excluded from the jury list since such persons were usually excused on a claim of hardship. Such a panel was held unfairly drawn and a new trial ordered.

[49] Thiel v. Southern Pac. Ry. Co., *supra* n. 48 at 225.

[50] See Ballard v. United States, 329 U.S. 187, 193-195, 67 S.Ct. 261, 91 L.Ed. 181 (1946), 35 Calif. L. Rev. 461, 33 Va. L. Rev. 519 (1946).

[51] Fay v. New York, 332 U.S. 261, 67 S.Ct. 1613, 91 L.Ed. 2043 (1947), 47 Colum. L. Rev. 463, 33 Conn. L.Q. 272, 46 Mich. L. Rev. 262 (1947). Mr. Justice Jackson, speaking for the Court, said: "The defendants have shown no intentional and purposeful exclusion of any class, and they have shown none that was prejudicial to them. . . . The function of this federal court under the Fourteenth Amendment in reference to state juries is not to prescribe procedures but is essentially to protect the integrity of the trial process. . . . The jury system is one which has undergone great modification in its long history . . . and it is still undergoing revision and adaptation to adjust it to the tensions of time and locality. . . ." 332 U.S. at 294, 295. See also Scott, *The Supreme Court's Control Over State and Federal Juries*, 34 Iowa L. Rev. 577 (1949).

[52] See Meltzer, *supra* n. 1.

[53] 67 A.B.A. Rep. 559 (1938). See also Vanderbilt, *op. cit. supra* n. 34 at 147-162.

those who carry their notions of "democracy" and equality to the extreme of asserting (1) that everyone has a right to be a juror, and (2) that a litigant or an accused has the right to have a jury chosen at random from the populace. But if we look at the administration of justice as a practical matter vitally concerned with affairs touching intimately the welfare both of private citizens and the state, can we possibly say that there is a place on the jury for convicts, the illiterate, or persons mentally or physically unfit? Obviously not, if justice is to be done, yet there are places where the "democratic" process of selecting jurors solely from the voting registers prevails.[54]

Sound standards for qualification of jurors were recommended in the report of Judge Knox's Committee to the Judicial Conference:

> "I. In order that grand and petit jurors to serve in United States district courts may be so drawn as to be truly representative of the community, the sources from which they are selected should include all economic and social groups of the community. From whatever sources they are drawn, those chosen should possess as high a degree of intelligence, morality, integrity, and common sense as can be found by those who make the selection. . . ."[55]

The revision in 1948 of Title 28 of the United States Code gave effect in Sections 1861 and 1862 with some exceptions to the recommendations of the Knox Report with respect to the qualifications and exemptions of jurors. The principal exception is that no person may be a federal juror who is incompetent to serve as a grand or petit juror by the law of the state in which the district court is held.[56] This adherence to the principle of conformity continues to expose the federal courts to all the vagaries of state practice as to qualifications of jurors and as to exemptions from jury duty. In the states,

> ". . . the varied regulations as to qualifications may be classified as those relating to: (1) citizenship and eligibility as a voter; (2) residence in the locality; (3) ownership of certain property, or payment of taxes; (4) minimum and maximum age limits; (5)

---

[54] Judge Knox's comment on such an experiment in his court is illuminating: *Jury Selection*, 22 N.Y.U.L.Q. REV. 433, 437-438 (1947).

[55] The Committee on Selection of Jurors consisted of Judges Neblett, Lindley, Procter, Watkins and Knox as Chairman, was appointed in September, 1941 and made its Report to the Judicial Conference of Senior Circuit Judges in 1942. This Recommendation is reprinted in VANDERBILT, *op. cit. supra* n. 34 at 151. See also Otis, *Selecting Federal Court Jurors*, 29 A.B.A.J. 19-21 (1943) arguing that jurors must be selected for their intelligence and ability to perform their tasks adequately and that not everybody is competent to serve.

[56] 28 U.S.C.A. sec. 1861 (4) rejected the recommendation of the Knox Report that liberal uniform standards be established for all federal jurors "leaving to the district judges a large degree of discretion in determining whether or not certain individuals or classes should be subject to jury service." Report at 6. See also *An Analysis of Alternative Constructions of the Requirement that Federal Jurors be Competent Under State Law*, 64 YALE L.J. 1059 (June 1955).

general health, ability to see and hear, and to serve generally; (6) sex; (7) mental ability and intelligence of the juror, i.e., the capacity for speaking and understanding English, education and native intelligence; (8) character, morals and a criminal record; (9) membership in a specified group or class; (10) prior service and requests for service. This classification indicates only the general spheres in which there is regulation. The mere listing of these classes cannot create a true picture of the complicated variations of these requirements for qualification as a juror in each state. This is an impossibility."[57]

The exemptions from jury duty in the several states vary as widely as the qualification for service, so as to make classification almost hopeless:

"These exemptions bear witness not only to the varied necessities of life in the United States, but also the inventiveness and ingenuity of the state legislatures and to the pressures exerted by the various groups that have obtained exemptions. In many states, moreover, persons classified as exempt are in reality disqualified since they are eliminated from the final jury list, although in nine states the names of those qualified but known to be exempt are placed on the final jury list. Among the classes of exemptions that may be defined are those applying to: (1) persons practicing certain professions considered vital or valuable to the public (including veterinaries and embalmers, etc., as well as members of the legal and medical profession); (2) persons engaged in certain businesses or trades where private and public interest require they should not be taken from their employment (including such persons as printers, millers, ferry-boat men and bank tellers); (3) specified governmental officials and employees in government departments of particular public interest (post office employees, firemen, policemen, and the like); (4) women; (5) persons of certain ages; (6) persons who have served once already within a certain period; and (7) particular named classes because of special private hardship. Persons may also be excused temporarily because of emergencies of one sort or another causing particular hardship at that time. This summary of the varieties of exemptions allowed in the several states indicates somewhat the complexities of the statutory picture and demonstrates that exemptions are most frequently accorded to those persons having the most education and experience, thus probably intensifying the difficulties attached to the problem of securing competent persons as jurors who represent a 'cross-section' of the community."[58]

As a result of these state regulations as to the qualifications and exemptions "millions of persons, possessing the best and most intelligent brains in all the land, are relieved, by law, of the necessity of lending

---

[57] VANDERBILT, *op. cit. supra* n. 34 at 163-171. See *id.* n. 62-75 for statutory provisions of particular states.

[58] *Id.* at 171-181. See *id.* at n. 76-86 for statutory provisions of particular states.

aid to the courts in their search for justice."⁵⁹ The limitation of exemptions to the six classes recommended by the Knox report—"The illiterate, criminals, the infirm, public officials, members of the armed services in active service and those who have performed jury service within two preceding years"⁶⁰—would have been far more satisfactory.

In addition to whatever exemptions are permitted to certain classes by statute, it is essential that power be given to "each district judge to grant such additional exemptions or excuses for classes or individuals as may be necessary to suit conditions within his district,"⁶¹ for as Judge Knox has demonstrated there are many citizens outside of the classes now exempted by statute from jury duty who should be excused, especially those who have to come long distances, proprietors of one-man business enterprises to whom jury service would mean ruination, and those who cannot afford to do jury duty.⁶²

### 3. Selection of Jurors

The next consideration relates to the manner in which juries are selected. The greatest evil in jury selection is politics. A corrupt or biased jury can nullify the work of the ablest judge and lawyers. In those countries where the jury lists are made up by a politically elected official, it is almost inevitable that the juries will reflect in their personnel the prevailing political influences in a manner incompatible with the fair administration of justice. In counties where partisan spirit is not so intense, the results may not be so harmful, but the danger is always there. I remember as a young lawyer when juries were still selected by the sheriff,⁶³ my surprise at the differences from county to county in the appearance, caliber and conduct of juries. I also remember years later, when as chairman of the Judicial Council of my state I was advocating a bill giving the judiciary the power to appoint jury commissioners to make up the jury lists, the willingness of a prominent party leader, later a United States senator, to support the bill if it could be applied to juries in civil cases only, but his opposition to the measure if it applied to grand juries or trial juries in criminal cases. He frankly told

---

⁵⁹ Knox, *supra* n. 54 at 437. See also for criticism of the various exemptions and the effect of such exemptions on securing competent jurors, Broeder, *supra* n. 14, 390 (1954).
⁶⁰ REPORT 42 (1942).
⁶¹ *Id.* at 3.
⁶² Knox, *supra* n. 54. This has been accomplished by statute for the federal courts. 28 U.S.C.A. sec. 1863. The compensation of jurors is also an important element in effective jury service. A recent amendment to the U.S. Code, 28 U.S.C.A. sec. 1871, increased the per diem fee to $7.00 and also allowed an increased fee if the case ran over 30 days.
⁶³ As to the 17th century recognition of the importance of the sheriff because of his powers to select juries and of the difference in juries chosen by sheriffs of different political persuasions see Havighurst, *supra*, n. 13.

me that as a politician he would not like to lose the right to a friendly grand jury or trial jury in a criminal suit "just in case." Justifiably, therefore, the first recommendation of the American Bar Association is "That jurors should be selected by commissioners appointed by the courts."[64] The judges who constituted the Knox Committee concurred in this by their recommendation that the "final responsibility and choice of means of selecting jurors rest with each district judge; ... the names of all prospective jurors must be chosen under the direction of the court by a jury commission, consisting of the clerk and jury commissioners."[65]

In the federal courts, the clerk, who is appointed by the court, and another jury commissioner of the opposite political party from the clerk's, likewise appointed by the court, attend a jury selection.[66] Although in many states jury commissioners do select jurors, in sixteen states or parts thereof county officers or the governing county boards make the choice, and in eight states or parts thereof the mayors or local governing boards make up the jury lists. In three states the governor and in twenty-four states a court appoints the jury commissioners. In nine states the judges themselves make up the jury lists. In Pennsylvania two of the three jury commissioners in each county (the third being a judge) are elected. And in some states the modes of selection often differ in various parts of a state.[67]

The appointment of jury commissioners by the judges is the best possible method of selection because it places the responsibility for obtaining efficient jurors where it should be imposed—within the judicial system. But even the desirability of this method is subject in every instance to two collateral inquiries: first, are the appointing judges out of politics; and, second, are the appointing power and the supervising power (which may or may not be the same) really impressed with the importance of proper jury selection to the due administration of justice and therefore willing to give the matter the time and thought it deserves and requires? Moreover, the jury commissioners themselves must be alive to the importance of the role that citizens play as jurors in the administration of justice and they must be determined to give their communities the best juries possible under the standards set up by law.[68]

Having considered who is qualified for or exempt from service and who is to select the jury panels, the next question is, how are the jury commissioners to select the panels of prospective jurors from among those eligible for such responsibilities? This goes to the heart of getting

---

[64] 63 A.B.A. REP. 563 (1938), VANDERBILT, *op. cit. supra* n. 34 at 185.
[65] REPORT (1942) Recommendation IV at 6.
[66] 28 U.S.C.A. sec. 1864.
[67] VANDERBILT, *op. cit. supra* n. 34 at 185-189.
[68] See Hernandez v. Texas, 347 U.S. 475, 74 S.Ct. 667, 98 L.Ed. 866 (1954) discussed in Lecture I, n. 5 *supra*.

effective juries. Selection, as we have seen, is essential in both metropolitan and rural areas. The only directions as to selection set up in the federal statutes is that grand and petit jurors shall be selected "from such parts of the district as the court directs so as to be most unfavorable to an impartial trial, and not to incur unnecessary expense or unduly burden the citizens of any part of the district with jury service."[69] This leaves the federal district judges free to follow the standards of selection recommended in the Knox report.[70] How these standards are to be applied is dealt with concretely in the second recommendation of the Knox report:

"II. The choice of specific sources from which names of prospective jurors are selected must be entrusted to the good faith of the clerk and jury commissioner, acting under the direction of the district judge, but should be controlled by the following considerations: (1) the sources should be so coordinated as together to include all groups in the community; (2) economic and social status including race and color should be considered only to the extent necessary to assure that there is no discrimination on account of them; (3) when women are eligible by law for jury service, they should be selected and called to serve in the Federal courts; (4) political affiliation should be ignored; (5) unsolicited requests of persons who seek to have their names placed upon jury lists and unsolicited recommendations of names should not be recognized; and (6) in determining the parts of the districts from which jurors are to be drawn (U.S.C., Title 28, sec. 413) the courts should bear in mind the desirability of conserving the time of jurors and preventing exorbitant travel expense to the government."[71]

With the federal practice is to be compared the Cleveland system recommended by the American Bar Association:

"The jury system used in Cleveland was recommended for adoption in other metropolitan centers. Its main feature is the key-number system. The registration list of voters forms the basis of the jury list. The number of jurors required for the year is estimated by the court, and to this is added a number equal to that which past experience has shown probably will be eliminated upon examination. The resultant figure is divided into the entire list of voters, the quotient then being used as a key number in selecting jurors' names from the polling list. The citizens whose names have been chosen according to the key number are required to answer questionnaires, then are summoned to appear before the jury commissioners and be personally examined, until the requisite number of prospective jurors is selected. The purpose of the examination is to secure jurors who are 'physically and mentally healthy, possessing good

---

[69] 28 U.S.C.A. sec. 1865 (a).
[70] KNOX REPORT (1942) Recommendation I, quoted herein (text preceding n. 55).
[71] *Id.* at 5. See also Knox, *supra* n. 54 at 441.

reputation for honesty and morality; with at least enough education to be able to read, write and understand English; and finally of sufficient intelligence and experience in life to be able to understand the various problems presented in both civil and criminal litigation.' "[72]

Questionnaires to prospective jurors and personal interviews with them as emphasized in the Cleveland plan were likewise recomended in the Knox report.[73] While the federal statutes are silent on the subject, there is nothing to prevent the federal district judges from prescribing questionnaires and personal interviews as recommended. Both questionnaires and personal interviews are essential to effective jury selection. Where questionnaires and personal interviews are regularly used, the Cleveland plan and the federal practice come out very much to the same end—the ideal stated by the Knox committee. Whether these ideals are attained depends primarily on the trial judge.

The Cleveland system has not found acceptance except in Ohio, Los Angeles, San Francisco, Pittsburgh, and some counties of Nebraska.[74] How then are prospective jurors selected in other places?

> "The officials making the selection for the jury panel, relying in part on their own knowledge, in eighteen jurisdictions select names at random or from those referred to them by others or from various sources, such as the assessor's roll or tax list, the poll list or voter's registry, the telephone and city directories, and other lists such as census reports, while attempting to secure a proportional geographical distribution of the jurors.

> "Before the names are placed on the final jury list or placed in a jury wheel, an investigation is made in twenty jurisdictions to determine whether the prospective juror meets the statutory qualifications, also has qualities of intelligence, experience, education, etc., that would make him a satisfactory juror. Nine states investigate the prospective juror only to determine whether he meets the statutory qualifications or is exempt. Two states only determine whether the juror has the statutory qualifications. The investigation or determination with respect to a juror's qualifications, exemptions and qualities is based on the personal knowledge of those selecting the jurors in ten states. California's system of investigation authorizes a combination of personal interviews, written examinations, questionnaires and intelligence tests. In Missouri this is done in the larger cities. Questionnaires are used in the District of Columbia and Connecticut, while personal interviews are combined with the use of a questionnaire in the Detroit Recorder's Court and in Massachusetts as well as in Cleveland. In New York City inter-

---

[72] VANDERBILT, *op. cit. supra* n. 34 at 148-149.
[73] Recommendation V, KNOX REPORT at 7. See also VANDERBILT, *op. cit. supra* n. 34 at 181-185.
[74] *Id.* at 189.

views, questionnaires, and inquiry of others are utilized. Personal interviews may be relied on in five states, while in five more inquiry of others is relied on solely.

"It is apparent from this that, while ostensibly an investigation is made in most states as to the competency of the prospective juror, in only a few has there been any attempt to do this in a scientific or businesslike fashion. For the most part reliance on personal information or inquiry of others is the basis of the determination, and such traditional methods can hardly be considered efficient in these days of increasing congestion and mobility of population."[75]

A jury list having been prepared, wisely or otherwise, the next step is to draw from it enough names to serve the court in its current sessions. This is also done in various ways in the different states.[76] After the panel of prospective qualified jurors have been selected, they are notified to appear in court, either by a summons or by registered mail.[77] Upon their appearance in the courtroom the ultimate selection of the trial jurors begins. In the United States where the newspapers and other media of communication fully discuss and comment on civil and criminal suits prior to and during trial,[78] a preliminary examination seems essential to determine the attitudes of jurors whose background and individual prejudices cannot otherwise possibly be known for an effective utilization of the challenge for cause and peremptory challenges accorded the parties by law. A juror is considered impartial within the requirements of the Sixth Amendment if he states he is able to decide a case on the evidence presented in the court, even if he has formed an opinion as to the case as a result of pretrial publicity.[79] The ability of the average prospective juror untrained in the act of judgment not to allow such preconceived opinions to color his reception of the evidence is subject to question. Such a juror is not subject to challenge for cause, however, although there is nothing to prevent the defendant from

---

[75] *Id.* at 181-185.
[76] For details of particular states' practice see *id.* at 189-194.
[77] *Id.* at 194-195; 28 U.S.C.A. sec. 1867. The period of jury service may vary from one week to a month, a term of court, or a year.
[78] This is in contrast to England where newspaper comment on judicial proceedings is severely restricted. See Goodhart, Newspapers and Contempt of Court in English Law, 48 HARV. L. REV. 885 (1935). For discussion of American attitude toward use of the contempt power to control prejudicial publications see FORER, *A Free Press and a Fair Trial*, 39 A.B.A.J. 800 (1953); for discussion of the respective claims to a free and a fair trial see Otterbourg, *Fair Trial and Free Press: A New Look in 1954*, 40 A.B.A.J. 838 (1954); Note, *Due Process for Whom—Newspaper or Defendant*, 4 STAN. L. REV. 101 (1951). See also Bibliography, *Trial by Newspaper* in Phillips and McCoy, CONDUCT OF JUDGES AND LAWYERS 187 (1952).
[79] See Note, *The Right to an Impartial Federal Jury and the Effect of Prejudicial Pretrial Publicity*, 53 COLUM. L. REV. 651, 653 (1953) for questions which may be asked in order to determine bias.

using his peremptory challenge to exclude such a juror. "The challenge for cause and its companion device the peremptory challenge are primarily designed to secure an impartial jury by the elimination of unduly prejudiced jurymen. While challenges for cause permit rejection of prospective jurors on the ground of provable and legally cognizable evidence of partiality, peremptories permit further rejection for real or imagined partiality that is less easily designated and proved."[80] The mode of use of challenges is regulated by statute in some states and otherwise is left to the discretion of the trial court. In all jurisdictions, a certain number of peremptory challenges are probably allowed and an unlimited number of challenges for cause.[81] Challenges for cause include challenges for relationship to the parties, interest in the outcome of the case, for being actually hostile or so prejudiced as to be unable to be impartial, or on the ground of statutory lack of qualifications as where a prospective juror cannot speak English if this is required, or is not a citizen, etc. Peremptory challenges do not require assignment of any reason and may be exercised freely by the party, without regard to cause.[82]

In England, the common law rule never authorized a preliminary examination of jurors upon their appearance in court before they were challenged. Challenges have rarely been used there, and only if used, is there any *voir dire* examination of a juror.[83] While originally the common law practice may have been transferred to America, early in the history of the United States the practice developed of having a preliminary examination in the court to select jurors from the panel, and to determine the acceptability and partiality of a juror, and the basis, if any, for a challenge. Before a challenge is made, in contrast to England, it became usual for the lawyers to interrogate the members of the jury panel to determine their suitability. This may have been in recognition of the greater powers of judgment entrusted to American jurors, which made their opinions so important, together with the difficulties in the early settlements of knowing well or much about your constantly migrating neighbor, as well as being a part of the curtailment of the

---

[80] Note, *Selection of Jurors by Voir Dire Examination and Challenge*, 58 YALE L.J. 638 (1949).

[81] The timing and order of taking challenges can be a matter of importance to attorneys, see *id.* 642-644. In civil cases from two to five peremptory challenges are generally permitted and in criminal cases the number varies from two to more than twenty. The defendant is usually given more than the prosecution. *Id.* at 639 n. 8.

[82] As to the manner of their use see Bodin, Selecting a Jury 20-50 (Prac. Law Instit. Trial Practice rev. 1948).

[83] HOWARD, CRIMINAL JUSTICE IN ENGLAND 362-363 (1931); MILLAR, CIVIL PROCEDURE OF THE TRIAL COURT 289-292 (1952); ORFIELD, CRIMINAL PROCEDURE FROM ARREST TO APPEAL 355 (1947).

activities of the trial judge and consequent increase in the initiative of the attorneys in the case.[84]

Today it is recognized that only if the conduct of the *voir dire* is entrusted to the judge can the various abuses of this questioning which have developed over the years be eliminated and undue delay in such examinations and the possible demoralization of the jurors be avoided. In criminal actions where the examination of jurors is conducted by the attorneys, it is often so lengthy as to be unduly expensive to the State as well as needlessly delaying the trial.[85] In ten states the *voir dire* examination of the jurors is conducted by the judge alone.[86] In eleven states the examination is conducted by the attorneys alone.[87] In the remaining states, either the practice provided by the federal procedural rules which authorized the judges to conduct the examination or to allow the attorneys or parties to do so is specifically incorporated in the state procedure or the oral questioning customarily is conducted by the judges and attorneys.[88]

The *voir dire* examination which is the basis for the challenges may be used by lawyers as an opportunity to influence or prejudice the entire jury[89] panel rather than being used for its basic aim, the production of an impartial jury. Where, however, the *voir dire* is conducted by the judge, the opportunity to abuse the jurors is eliminated and the choices of securing an unprejudiced jury are enhanced. While the right to challenge the jury as a whole or a juror in particular should admittedly not be restricted if the aim of a jury trial is to see that justice is to be done rather than to accord one party an advantage over another by

---

[84] MILLAR, *op. cit. supra* n. 83 at 292-293; PUTTKAMMER, ADMINISTRATION OF CRIMINAL LAW 175-182 (1953). Puttkammer notes that the homogeneousness of the English population and the property qualification for jury service there make it less significant who is chosen than in the United States where the prospective jury is selected from a more varied population.

[85] ORFIELD, *op. cit. supra* n. 83 at 401-404.

[86] VANDERBILT, *op. cit. supra* n. 34 at 198-200. See also MILLAR, *op. cit. supra* n. 83 at 293-294. As to discretion of court as to question asked on *voir dire* see Frederick v. United States, 163 Fed. 536 (9th Cir. 1947), Kopysincski v. Farrar et al., 63 F. Supp. 857 (ND 1946), appeal dismissed, 155 F.2d 725 (8th Cir. 1946).

[87] See Note, 58 YALE L.J. 638, 640 n. 10 as to latitude of questioning permitted lawyers during *voir dire*.

[88] FED. RULES CIV. PRO. 47; FED. RULES CRIM. PRO. 24a, MILLAR, *op. cit. supra* n. 83 at 289-297; VANDERBILT, *op. cit. supra* n. 34 at 197-200.

[89] See GOLDSTEIN, TRIAL TECHNIQUE 152-194 (1935). The author observes the need of the trial lawyer to "sell both his client and himself into the good graces of the jury" and that "In most cases it is found the jury tries the lawyers rather than the clients." At 152.

To similar effect it has been said that in addition to laying the foundation for the elimination of prejudicial jurors "The voir dire, however, also affords counsel an opportunity to educate the jury on the issues in the case, to stifle inclination towards prejudice which are not definite enough to warrant the elimination of jurors, and to lay the foundation for the development of strategy and tactics. This opportunity is extremely important and should not be overlooked." Bodin, *op. cit. supra* n. 82 at 1.

reason of the presence of the jury, no excuse can be found for the prolongation of the *voir dire* by leaving it to the control of attorneys no matter how skillful they may be. If the aim is to secure an impartial jury, there is more reason for the examination of the jury to be conducted by the court who is impartial than to leave it to attorneys who are bound to attempt to use every opportunity they may have, to secure a favorable jury rather than to secure an impartial one.

### 4. Status of the Jury in England and in the United States

Before the Judicature Acts of 1873-1875 the normal mode of trial at common law in England was by judge and jury. Under the Judicature Acts trial by jury fell off markedly "from 1885 until 1917, roughly one half of all cases heard in the King's Bench Division were before a judge alone."[90] In 1917 the shortage of manpower led to restrictive measures which were not repealed until 1925, but notwithstanding the repealer the popularity of the jury continued to decline, hastened by restrictions imposed in 1933, with the result that in 1940 jury trials were had in less than ten percent of the civil cases in the King's Bench Division. Although the restriction on juries was lifted in 1947, the percentage of jury trials in 1949 dropped still further to slightly over three percent of the cases tried in the King's Bench Division.[91] "Whether or not there will be a jury in a civil action is therefore now a matter for the discretion of the judge, as it was before 1939."[92]

Various causes have been suggested for this decline in the popularity of trial by jury in civil cases in England: the general infusion of the spirit of equity into the law after the Judicature Acts, the disappearance of the often overbearing judges of the eighteenth century with the resultant growth of popular confidence in the judiciary; the heavy costs imposed on the losing party in a jury case; and the savings of time and energy by trial without a jury. Perhaps the greatest detriment to jury trials is the dark shadow of heavy costs that will be assessed against the loser. Costs everywhere are the one black spot in the administration of English justice, for the costs resulting from the loss of a single case may ruin a man financially.[93] In criminal cases the situation is

---

[90] JACKSON, *op. cit. supra* n. 44 at 64. For detailed analysis see JACKSON, *The Incidence of Jury Trial During the Past Century*, 1 MODERN L. REV. 132 (1937).
[91] *Ibid.*
[92] "This is clearly shown in Christen v. Goodacre (1949) W.N. 234; in an action against a house surgeon for damages for negligence in surgical treatment the judge ordered trial by jury notwithstanding the fact that the hospital authorities who were co-defendants did not want jury trial, and that the case involved scientific and medical evidence and difficult legal questions; the Court of Appeal refused to interfere with the judge's discretion." Material furnished to the editor by Prof. Jackson.
[93] "It is probable that the appointment of the present committee (on Practice

quite different. If the defendant is proceeded against by indictment and pleads not guilty, there must be a trial by jury. Since the war the tendency has been to prosecute by indictment rather than by proceedings before a magistrate because of the heavier penalties that may be imposed in a trial by indictment. Accordingly, in criminal matters the proportion of cases tried by jury in England has risen in recent years.[94]

In this country the jury has suffered no such decline in popularity as it has in England. Yet even the stoutest defenders of the jury system are frank to admit that it is far from perfect in operation. The conviction that the efficiency of jury trials must be increased if their basic purpose is to be effectuated and if they are not to be discarded completely underlies the various suggestions for reform of jury practice and in the selection of a jury. The efficiency of jury trials depends as much on the caliber of the juror as on the character and training of the trial judges and the powers accorded the judge in the conduct of jury trials.

The contemporary criticisms of the jury are not superficial but have substantial foundations. Nevertheless, it may be said irrevocably that the jury forms such a fundamental part of American practice and represents, even if it does not satisfy, a desire for popular participation in the judicial process that it is not likely that the jury will ever fall into such disuse in this country as in England.[95] But if juries are to be used most satisfactorily not even the staunchest apologist for them will deny that some reforms in jury practice and in the qualifications and selection for jury service are essential. Despite the demand in time and energy and the cost of juries, jury service should be recognized as a

---

and Procedure) was due in large part to the libel action which the late Professor Harold Laski brought against the Daily Express. He lost the action, with the result that he had to pay not only his own costs, but also the costs of his opponents which were taxed at about £5,000, which at that time meant $20,000 When it became known that he might have to sell his Library so as to pay these costs, a public subscription was started. This led to the feeling that the cost of litigation in England was so great as to amount virtually to a denial of justice in some cases. . . ."

"In a recent case which concerned an unimportant right-of-way across a small farm the costs which the loser had to pay his opponent exceeded £2,000. These did not include the costs he had to pay to his own solicitor, counsel, and witnesses. Where the amount at stake in a case is a large one the English system is not an unsatisfactory one, but where the amount at stake is small, the loser may find that, without any fault on his part, he has been ruined by insisting on his day in court." Goodhart, *Current Judicial Reform in England*, 27 N.Y.U.L. REV. 395, 397, 406 (1952). The final and detailed report of the (Evershed) Committee on Supreme Court Practice and Procedure, was issued in July, 1953. For consideration of its major findings see Gower, *The Cost of Litigation*, 17 MODERN L. REV. 1 (1954).

[94] Letter of Prof. Jackson to the editor written Jan. 11, 1952.
[95] See BOK, *The Jury System in America*, 287 ANNALS 92 (1953).

civic responsibility, which all should assume and not attempt to avoid.[96] The exemptions from jury service should be narrowed so that many well qualified classes will not be excluded. The need to supply competent jurors is basic. The *voir dire* must be merely an opportunity to obtain an impartial jury and not a chance for forensic pyrotechnics. Above all, the relationship of judges and jurors must be regularized so that the judge may assist the jury by commenting on the evidence and devices must be experimented with to aid the jury to best perform its prime function of fact determination. The use of jurors puts the case before the bar of public opinion and makes possible the desirable community determination of the right and wrong of the case. The presence of lay judges in many European courts and the many powers entrusted to this day to the lay English justices of the peace are indicative of an almost universal recognition that in the trial of certain disputes the presence of a lay element is of great importance. But the lay element cannot function without judicial guidance as to the law; if the administration of justice in the courts is to be based on law the respective functions and responsibilities of both judge and jury must be clearly recognized.[97]

---

[96] As to the importance of making jury service more attractive see OSBORN, THE MIND OF THE JUROR 168-171 (1937).

[97] "Almost all of the problems of jurisprudence come down to a fundamental one of rule and discretion, of administration of justice by law and administration of justice by the more or less trained intuition of experienced magistrates . . . both are necessary elements in the administration of justice. . . ." POUND, AN INTRODUCTION TO THE PHILOSOPHY OF LAW 54 (Rev. ed. 1954).

# INDEX

Act of Settlement, 17
Admiralty courts, jury not used, 57-58
Administration of justice, judicial duties, 11-12
Air space, change in law of, 4
Alabama, selection of judges, 46-47
American Bar Association: Canons of Judicial Ethics, 28; minimum standards for administration of justice, 11; recommendations on judicial instruction of juries, 60; recommendation on jury selection, 68-69; recommendation on regulation of procedure, 11; Section of Judicial Administration, Committee on Selection of Jurors, 64
American Law Institute; Restatement of the Law, 5
Appellate courts, purpose of review, 4
Attaint, writ of, 53

Bi-partisan selection of judges, 39, 49-50
Bracton, on King and law, 13
*Bushell's Case,* 53-54

California; jury selection, 70; selection of judges, 46
Canons of Judicial Ethics, 28-29
Challenges, usage, 71-72
Chancery, development, 16
Chicago, partisan politics and judicial selection, 41-42
Chief justice, responsibility for court administration, 12
Civil law, conception of courts and judges, 13, 47
Cleveland, jury selection, key number system, 69-70
Code, regulation of procedure by, 11
*Code of Civil Procedure,* Field, 11
*Code of Jackson,* 13
Coke; on property rights in air space, 4; on supremacy of law, 13-14
Common law, development and extensiveness of, 4-5
Connecticut; jury selection, 70
Constitution; grand jury provision, 52; jury trial, 56, 62

Contrast; judicial profession, 47
Courts: admiralty in American colonies, 57; appellate, purpose of review, 4; England, development of royal, 14; federal, jury selection in, 68; importance of personnel, 2; role of, 1; traffic, importance of, 10; weaknesses of, 2

Declaration of Independence: on judge, 21, on jury, 57
Delaware, bipartisan appointment of judges, 39
Denning, Mr. Justice, on rule of law and independence of judiciary, 18
Detroit Recorder's Court, jury selection, 70
District of Columbia, jury selection, 70

Election of judges; change to in U.S., 36; partisan pressures in, 40-45
England: costs, heaviness of, 74; courts, development of royal, 14; judicial office, development, 15; judicial selection, 26-27, 32-35; judicial tenure, 14-17; jury challenges, 72; jury origins and development, 51-55; jury practices, 60; jury qualifications, 62; jury use, 74; legal profession, evolution, 14-17; nonpartisan selection of judges, 48; philosophy of judicial office, 13; rule of law, 18

Federal Rules of Procedure, Success of, 12
Field Code of Civil Procedure, 11
France, judiciary, 47

George III, effectuation of judicial independence during reign, 14, 18
Grand Jury, importance, 52

Hand, Chief Justice Learned; on government of laws and men, 3; on judges and development of law, 5

Immunity, common law doctrine of, 20

# INDEX

Jackson, Justice, 12
Jacksonian Revolution; changes in judicial selection and tenure, 36; enlargement of jury powers, 58
Jay, Chief Justice, 12
Jewett, Lord Chancellor, on selection of judges, 34
Judges: administration of justice, responsibilities for, 11; administrative duties, 12; American, colonial, 19; Anglo-American, not public servants, 2; attributes of good, 26-30; character and personality, importance, 2; development of law, 4; England, 14-17, 26-27, 32-35, 48; functions of, 1, 3-13; immunity, impartiality, independence, 17, 19-20, 50; judicial review, 11; jury relationship, 3, 6-7, 57-59, 60-62, 73, 76; non-judicial governmental assignments of, 12; political experience of, 50; professional competence, 26-28; regulation of judicial procedure, 11; selection of, see Selection of Judges, this Index; standards for, 31; tenure, see Judicial Tenure, this Index; trial, see Trial Judges, this Index; trial without a jury, 8; United States, 6-8, 10-12, 21-28, 35-46; voir dire examination, control of, 73
Judicial independence, 17, 19-20, 25-26
Judicial review, power of, 10
Judicial tenure; colonial complaints, 21; early U.S. provisions, 22; English achievement of secure, 14-17; federal provisions, 21-23; judicial independence, relation to, 25-26; life tenure, defense of, Chief Justice Marshall, 23-24; states, limited, 24-25
Jury: attaint, use of writ, 53; Bushell's Case, importance of, 53; challenges of, 71-72; commissioners for selection of, 68; common law trial, 51, 56-57; constitutional provisions for, 56, 62; criticisms of, 75-76; educational value of, 57; England, 60, 72, 74; exemptions from service in the states, 66-67; functions, 6, 51-62; general verdict, 59-61; grand, 52; impartiality, 63; instructions of, 7, 60; judge relationship and allocation of functions between, 3, 6-7, 55-59, 60-62, 70, 73, 76; origins of, 51; powers enlarged, 58; qualifications of, 62-66; reliance on in U.S., 56, 58; selection, 67-70; studies of, 64-65; trial, 52-53, 56, 58; U.S., use of, 62, 74-75; voir dire examination of, 71-74
*Justmen, Code of,* 13

Kent, Chancellor, on mode of selection of federal judges, 35
Knox, Chief Judge John C., jury study: recommendation for qualifications, 65; selection, 68-70

Legal Profession, England, evolution of, 14-17

*Marbury v. Madison,* 10
Marshall, Chief Justice, on judicial tenure, 23-24
Martin, Edward, *The Role of the Bar in Electing the Bench in Chicago,* 41-42
Massachusetts: constitutional provisions for judicial tenure, 22, 24; jury selection, 70
Missouri, judicial selection, 46; jury selection, 70
More, Chancellor, Sir Thomas, 16
Mott, Professor Rodney C., on measurement of judicial attributes, 31

New Hampshire: judicial selection, 39-40, judicial tenure, 24
New Jersey: bipartisan appointment of judges, 40, 48; judicial tenure, 24; traffic cases' importance, 10
New trial, judge's discretion in award of, 9
New York City, jury selection, 70-71

Parker, Chief Judge John J., on judicial independence, 19-20
Politics and selection of judges in U.S., 38-42

# INDEX

Pound, Dean Roscoe, on judges in civil law countries, 13
Precedent, binding force of, 4
Procedure, court regulation of, and statutory, 11

Restatement of the law, and the common law, 5
Rhode Island, judicial tenure in, 24
Roberts, Justice, 12
Royal prerogative, judicial function as part of, 15
Rule of law, development of, 14, 18

Selection of judges: ad interim appointment, importance of, 37; American Bar Association plan for, 46; appropriate methods, 47-49; bipartisan appointments, 39, 49-50; Continent, judicial profession, 47; elective system in U.S., 36, 42, 45; England, 32-33; federal, 35; partisan considerations, English disregard for, 34-35; political influence in U.S., 38-42, 45-47; present U.S. methods, 37
Sergeants, role in English legal development, 15-16
*Sparfe & Hansen v. United States,* 58
Special verdict and special interrogatories, 61
Statutes: judicial review, 10; regulation of procedure, 11
Stone, Chief Justice: on extra duties for judges, 12-13; on selection of judges, 44

Story, Justice, on functions of jury, 59
Stuarts, judicial appointments, manipulated by, 17
Supreme Court: appointments to, 38; on impartial jury, 63; rule making by, 11-12

Taft, William H. and Canons of Judicial Ethics, 28
Tocqueville, Alexis de: on educational value of jury, 57; on U.S. judicial review, 10-11
Traffic courts, importance of large number of cases in, 10
Trial: by Jury, see Jury herein; judicial control of processes of, 6; without a jury, 8
Trial Judge: common law powers of, 6; jury relationship, see Jury, this Index; finality of decisions of, 9-10; responsibilities of, 5-9; suggestions for changes in the law by, 4; trial without a jury, 6, 8

Unconstitutionality, judicial review of statutes for, 10
U.S. Code, Title 28, Revision, jury sections, 65

Vaughan, Chief Justice, in *Bushell's Case,* 53-54
Voir dire examination of jurors, 71-73

White, Chief Justice, on selection of judges, 50

| DATE DUE | |
|---|---|
| 5/4/07 | |
| | |
| | |
| | |
| | |
| | |
| | |
| | |
| | |
| | |
| | |
| | |
| | |
| | |
| | |
| | |
| | |
| | |
| GAYLORD | PRINTED IN U.S.A. |